*Endorsements*

"Prayer, honesty, and accountability are so important in the life of a believer. The women in my life who are my Fast Friends mean the world to me. What a great resource this book is!"

**FRANCESCA BATTISTELLI,** Christian music artist

"There is power when we devote ourselves to prayer. It can be more powerful when we pray with others in unity. *Fast Friends* is a reminder to make time for what matters most!"

**ALEX KENDRICK,** Writer and director of *War Room,*
*Courageous, Fireproof,* author of *The Love Dare*

"Niles and Little have taken Jesus' clear expectation that His followers would fast and have dropped it smack into the middle of our twenty-first century, frenetic, spiritually isolated, and all too often self-consumed world. It's clear these two Fast Friends have learned a thing or two about fasting and prayer through their shared experiences of discipline and mutual accountability, all within the context of their close friendship, and they winsomely share this wisdom through their personal testimonies in this book. I love that Suzanne and Wendy don't come off in these pages as lofty, pedantic experts, but rather as humble, down-to-earth, sister-travelers on this journey of faith and friendship, simply sharing what they have found to be key to their spiritual growth as women of God. An inspiring and motivating read!"

**MAJOR LISA SMITH,** The Salvation Army

"We establish friendships on shared interests, locale, hobbies, and much more. But it's rare to find a friendship forged through fasting and prayer. Suzanne and Wendy have woven a unique tapestry of compelling personal stories and rich biblical truth. Driven by a desire to see believers draw closer to the Lord and one another through these particular spiritual disciplines, this book will provide encouragement and support for all sorts of Fast Friends."

**MICHAEL CATT,** Senior pastor, Sherwood Baptist Church
Executive producer, Sherwood Pictures

" 'For where two or three gather in my name, there am I with them.' Suzanne and Wendy give us personal stories and great tips on how two girlfriends who love Jesus can rock the world. Thank you for inspiring the rest of us to seek an accountability partner, a friend and even a soul mate, to become more disciplined in our faith and more Christ-like in our lives. There is nothing more life changing than prayer and fasting and nothing more fun than walking that journey with a girlfriend. You go girls!"

**KAREN COVELL,** Producer and founding director
of The Hollywood Prayer Network
www.hollywoodprayernetwork.org

"*Fast Friends* is a sound reminder of the need for prayer—deep, costly, and committed—in a culture that would prefer individual and non-taxing expressions of commitment to God. The recommendations stemming from the authors' personal experience and understanding of Scripture will only help those wanting a deeper experience with the Lord in that quest."

**MATTHEW A. THOMAS,**
Bishop, Free Methodist Church, USA

"I believe God honors and listens when we get serious about renewing our minds, cleansing ourselves, and denying something in our lives that may be distracting us from following His lead. Books have been written about fasting, but Suzanne and Wendy have written a heartfelt and personal book that will make you laugh and help you understand that fasting should be focused but it can also be joyous and refreshing. There's merit in taking a fasting journey and this book will open your eyes to new and uplifting Godly insights that can transform your life."

**KATHLEEN COOKE,** VP Cooke Pictures and The Influence Lab,
kathleencooke.com

"I was hooked on *Fast Friends* by the end of the first paragraph. Delightful, fresh, and full of Bible truth, *Fast Friends* propelled me forward to look at my own prayer and fasting life and prepared me to dive into incorporating the principles into my own life. Suzanne and Wendy are living examples of what they have written. Their approach to Jesus is a daily walk of grace, hope, and purpose. Drawing near to God by their commitment to each other as Fast Friends has given them strength, wisdom, and transformed them to shine bright for Jesus."

**SHARI RIGBY,** Speaker and author of *Beautifully Flawed: Finding Your Radiance in the Imperfections of Your Life,* actress, *October Baby*

"*Fast Friends* is such an encouraging read! Suzanne and Wendy will inspire you with their tremendous love for the Lord and each other to search your heart and mind with their humble and biblical foundation to fasting and prayer."

**MARIA CANALS-BARRERA,** Actress, *God's Not Dead 2*

"*Fast Friends* is a valuable example of two ordinary women who said yes to an extraordinary God, and moved in obedience towards a journey of fasting and prayer. As Wendy and Suzanne learned more about the true condition of their own hearts, they submitted to the only One who could heal and transform their lives. I encourage you to ask God to bring you a Fast Friend. As you agree to enter into prayer and fasting you have the opportunity to deny yourself, only to ultimately gain more of Jesus!"

**KEVIN DOWNES,** Producer, actor, writer, *Faith of Our Fathers*,
*Mom's Night Out, Courageous*

"If you read this book and receive the challenge inside it, you will no doubt be changed for the better! You will be inspired towards a deeper intimacy with God and you will find that whatever you give up will be meaningless compared to all you gain! I have applied these principles to my life, and they have brought breakthrough in areas I never thought I'd conquer. I'm excited to share this wonderful work with my dear friends! Thank you, Suzanne and Wendy, for the triumph written on every page!"

**JENNIFER STRICKLAND,** Author, *Beautiful Lies*, urmore.org

"It is no small feat to cook up a compelling and delicious *feast* in a book about fasting, but Suzanne and Wendy deliver just such a treat in *Fast Friends*. The practical truths they share as their friendship grew and drew them closer to God offer hope for all of us. We all need *Fast Friends*."

**KEN ABRAHAM,** *New York Times* bestselling author

"In hard times our desire to be understood and loved is stronger than ever. We all need someone who will commit to pray and fast with us until the spiritual battle is won. I believe the biblical principles found in *Fast Friends* will supply comfort and hope in the midst of trials, as well as the supernatural power to fight the toughest storms. I encourage everyone to find a Fast Friend and enter your prayer closet and seek Jesus like never before!"

**ERICA GALINDO,** Founder and editor-in-chief,
SonomaChristianHome.com

"We found *Fast Friends* a book most worthy of our highest recommendation. We loved the backstory of how God knit Suzanne and Wendy together in both friendship and kingdom purposes. Their transparency and humility both blessed and challenged us in our own walks. We also loved the kingdom treasures that they mined through their determination to pursue God regularly for all that He wanted to do both in and through them. It was so affirming to learn about the ways God grew them in their relationship with Him and each other. It was then so easy to track how He magnified His power and victory in multiple areas of their lives. Since we both have experienced the very worthwhile kingdom fruit grown through fasting, we honor Suzanne and Wendy in this faithful effort to be all they can in and for the Lord in this very needy world."

**MARK FINCANNON,** Casting Director, C.S.A. *90 Minutes in Heaven*
**SHARON FINCANNON,** Casting Assistant, Fincannon Casting

"I've known Suzanne and Wendy for many years and they are vulnerable and transparent in this book from the heart on fasting and prayer. We all desire close community and someone we can count on to support us in both good times and bad. *Fast Friends* will inspire you to enter into the kind of meaningful relationship with a brother or sister in Christ where you carry one another's request before the throne. There are eternal benefits and a closer walk with the Savior to be garnered through *Fast Friends*. So what are you waiting for? Find your Fast Friend fast!"

**BOBBY DOWNES,** Cofounder and CEO
ChristianCinema.com

"In *Fast Friends*, Suzanne Niles and Wendy Simpson Little combine for a practical, yet intensely spiritual perspective on the age old question of fasting and how it works for them as contemporary women. A perfect guide for someone focused on the how-to's of fasting and the application to daily life."

**JOE BATTAGLIA,** President, Renaissance Communications and
author, *The Politically Incorrect Jesus*

"Want to fast and don't know the ropes? *Fast Friends* is the book for you. Here is a practical guide on prayer and fasting shared through the eyes of sisters in Christ. Suzanne Niles and Wendy Simpson Little bring to the forefront a topic that has long since been forgotten in our busy culture. God bless you both for your courage."

**SUELLEN ROBERTS,** Founder and president,
Christian Women in Media Association

"Suzanne and Wendy take the Bible seriously, and that's why I'm taking their book *Fast Friends* seriously. Even if you've never considered the impact fasting can have on your life, I encourage you to read it, and see how these insights can make a difference for you."

**PHIL COOKE,** Ph.D., Filmmaker, media consultant, and
author of *One Big Thing: Discovering What You Were Born to Do*

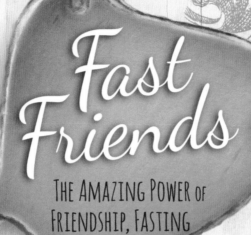

# Fast Friends

## The Amazing Power of Friendship, Fasting and Prayer

Suzanne Niles
and
Wendy Simpson Little

**BroadStreet**
PUBLISHING

BroadStreet Publishing Group, LLC
Racine, Wisconsin, USA
www.broadstreetpublishing.com

*Fast Friends*
THE AMAZING POWER OF FRIENDSHIP, FASTING, AND PRAYER

*Disclaimer: Before beginning any type of diet change or fasting, please consult with your doctor or medical professional. Some individuals will not be able to follow a regimen of fasting from food due to certain medical conditions.*

ISBN-13: 978-1-4245-5085-2 (hardcover)
ISBN-13: 978-1-4245-5086-9 (e-book)

Cover by Chris Garborg at www.garborgdesign.com
Interior by Katherine Lloyd at www.theDESKonline.com

Stock or custom editions of BroadStreet Publishing titles may be purchased in bulk for educational, business, ministry, fundraising, or sales promotional use. For information, please e-mail info@broadstreetpublishing.com

Printed in China

15 16 17 18 19 20 5 4 3 2 1

# Dedication

*We dedicate this book to our precious, powerful, loving Lord and Savior, Jesus Christ. We also dedicate it to you. God has placed this book in your hands so you can seek and know Him in a new way—one that will fill your heart to overflowing and help you step into everything He designed for you before the creation of the world.*

# Contents

# *Foreword*

There's not a friend like the lowly Jesus. Not one. But God knew, before the foundation of the world, that you and I, people that live on earth, would have a specific need to communicate with like kind, to bond with others, to have companionship, to relate with someone who could relate back to them. Oh what empathy and omnipotent majesty He has for his children! See Him work through these eternal friends from the pages of this book.

There is a song that encourages us that when we walk through a storm, we should hold our heads high and not be afraid of the storm. We, like the authors of this great work, have weathered many storms that have raged in our lives—grateful for an ear to listen, a tear to shed, an arm to lean on, a quick kick in the rear end (with love) when we whine, encouragement to hold on and not give up, and the triumph of success.

Do you realize the importance of praying to God for everything and realizing that someone is in one accord praying with you? Can you feel how lonely life is without a praying partner interceding for and with you? I do. There have been times in my life that I did not want people to know what I was praying about. Maybe they will think I'm silly, arrogant, hopeless, weak, dumb, powerless, a complainer, and a whiner? Or, maybe they will think I'm trying to be spiritual, religious, a Jesus freak, Holy Roller, and more?

As you saturate yourself in the fullness of this book, you will see the urgency of family and especially godly friendships where the super and the natural blend together over the trials and triumphs of life and together win the battles of life, which can be unseen and unexpected. By joining arm and arm with God-united friends and especially our Friend Jesus and walking together, even if we get weary physically, emotionally, spiritually, and economically, there's always a Friend that sticks closer than any brother. His name is Jesus. He will lead you through hard trials, tribulations, heartaches, and troubles as He keeps His word when He said, "I have overcome the world!"

Please let Him, the Author and Finisher of your faith, unite you to your Fast Friend who will join with you within the love of Jesus and will be there for you through thick and thin. Our joy should be in the Lord who created friendship in the beginning and has confirmed the process of friendships to the end of time, and will translate it into eternity where friendship will never end. My friend, you are in for a magnificent journey. Read and see!

Rev. Dr. Thelma Wells (Mama T),
Author, speaker, television personality, CEO
That A Girl & Friends Speakers Agency and Enrichment Tours
www.thatagirlspeakers.com
Women of Faith

# PART ONE

# Fixing the Focus

*Again I say to you, that if two of you agree on earth about anything that they may ask, it shall be done for them by My Father who is in heaven.*

—JESUS CHRIST (MATT. 18:19 NASB)

## CHAPTER 1

# Fast Friends from the Start

*W*e—Suzanne and Wendy—are fast friends. Between the two of us, we have worked as waitress, roller-rink hostess, data entry person, substitute teacher, missionary, file clerk, nanny, bra-fitter, campaign manager, writer, middle and high school teacher, actress, public relations manager, medical transcriptionist, executive secretary, real estate broker, and professional audio book recorder. We have also taught a wide array of subjects, including English, French, Tae Kwon Do, piano, acting, make up application, and Sunday school. We have sold videos, bras, cosmetics, jewelry, radon systems, and our own record album. We have sung for Jesus in foreign countries and for boisterous country crowds at state fairs. We have changed thousands of dirty diapers, wiped runny noses at least as many times, and smoothed away a million salty tears, often from our own faces. We have volunteered on more committees than we can remember and have had more specialized training on useless, inapplicable things than merits recording. We have met actors, politicians, musicians, apologists, and evangelists. We too have even engaged in a couple of those roles from time to time. We come from different backgrounds, different zip codes, different denominations, and have different dress sizes.

Still, in many important ways, which go beyond our paid-for blond hair and love of nachos, we are the same. We both adore Jesus. We ache for him to refine us through his love and power. We have no higher goal or ambition right now than to see Jesus be the root and foundation of our children's lives. And we pray and fast. And when our stomachs are growling from fasting, we pray and seek Him even more. Subsequently, we love Him even more.

Our story is far from fairytale. It has two very flawed heroines and a cast of other rambunctious characters. In fact, our favorite characters are our much-loved husbands and children. Our story takes place in two very different geographical settings: sunny central California and sometimes-sunny Spokane, Washington. It spans twelve years now, and it has a plot that seems a little convoluted at times but includes strong dramatic elements: sometimes comedic, sometimes tragic, yet strewn with glorious praises. Our story covers the sublime and the ridiculous, which you may have already gathered from the list of jobs we've had. We are not noteworthy, notable, or even note takers. We are more like the girls sitting in the back of the class comparing lipsticks and making plans for lunch—unless it's in a Bible study class. (Okay, we have been known to pass a note about lunch during Bible study too.)

As we tell you more of our story, we will encourage you to form a fast friendship. We want you to know how you can accept the invitation of the God of the universe—the invitation to spend close, intimate time with Him, offering Him your praise, getting your heart right with Him through repentance, and pouring out your concerns and needs to Him in prayer—and doing all of this with another sister in Christ.

So what you have in your hands is not a book of theology. Rather, this book is written out of our shared spiritual experience. God called us—two average women—to enter into a type of sisterhood that presented to us the opportunity to answer the cry of our hearts for a sincere and dedicated support system. God gave us a gift. The gift of a safe place of friendship where we meet Him, focus on Him, confess our sins to Him, worship Him, listen for His voice, and bring our most heartfelt requests before Him.

This relationship involves a good amount of prayer and some fasting too. While no Christian discounts the need for us to pray, we have heard some Christians claim that fasting is not for today. However, Jesus' instructions for how we are supposed to appear to others while fasting caused us to pause and think. Jesus said, "When you fast, do not look somber as the hypocrites do, for they disfigure their faces to show others they are fasting. Truly I tell you, they have received their reward in full. But when you fast, put oil on your head and wash your face, so that it will not be obvious to others that you are fasting, but only to your Father, who is unseen; and your Father, who sees what is done in secret, will reward you" (Matt. 6:16–18).

We became fixated on the fact that Jesus said *when* you fast, not *if*. We found that important in our research of whether or not fasting is for today. Jesus assumed that His hearers would fast, so He said, "When you fast," not "If you fast." Our study of this biblical passage and many others led us to conclude that fasting is not to be a spiritual discipline of the past; it is as relevant today as it was in Jesus' day. Granted, we did not find fasting commanded anywhere in the Bible. Nor did we come across any passage where God eliminated fasting. So what we concluded is that fasting is a choice, not a command. It is an elective discipline, not a divine demand. Yet, as a choice, it provides us with some rich opportunities. We found suffering some hunger pangs helped us live in greater abandonment to God, leading us deeper into our relationship with Him.

We understand that some people may be unable to engage in the fasting discipline because of certain health issues. If you are among this group, we don't want you to think that by not fasting you will somehow hinder yourself from living a more meaningful and surrendered life for Christ. Fasting is not a legalistic requirement; it is not a demand of divine law. Legalism has no place with us, much less in the Christian life described in Scripture. And for those who have trusted in Jesus Christ, there is no condemnation; He has set us free from the law (Rom. 8:1–2).

What we have discovered, however, is that when we seek God while fasting, He has revealed His perfect will for us. We're confident that He can do the same in other ways, but fasting is certainly one of those spiritual practices He honors in this way. (Just FYI, ladies, it may interest you that there is recent significant scientific evidence that fasting also has an anti-aging aspect because it allows your body a break. Just sayin'.)

Whether you choose to fast or not, you can rest in the fact

that God sees and knows the intent of your heart, and He will meet you at your own point of need.

Beyond our own needs, we also believe that God is stirring in the hearts of Christian women the desire to pray and fast as in the example of 2 Chronicles 7:14: "If my people, who are called by my name, will humble themselves and pray and seek my face and turn from their wicked ways, then I will hear from heaven, and I will forgive their sin and will heal their land." We think we all can agree that if ever there was a time our land needed healing, it is now. In order to fulfill the Great Commission and share the gospel of Jesus Christ with a lost and hurting world, we must pray and seek the Lord as never before.

Prayer and fasting change lives. They have changed our lives, and they can change yours too. And when we make these disciplines part of our lives and engage in them for the sake of others too, we can see their effect move far beyond our own worlds.

Is this what you want? Do you want to begin a journey of complete dependence, personal denial and sacrifice, willingness to have your sin revealed to you, and humility in confession before the Lord? To feel that cleansing that comes from His immediate forgiveness as promised in 1 John 1:9, "If we confess our sins, he is faithful and just and will forgive us our sins and purify us from all unrighteousness"? Do you love others enough to do spiritual battle on your knees on their behalf? Can you decide to be in agreement with another believer and God, to stay the course even when it is hard, so that you can ultimately come away with a greater devotion to God and His kingdom? Does your heart cry for more of Him and less of you? If your answer is yes to any of these questions, then your heart beats in time with ours. We have made the decision to pray and fast and do this work of love together. Will you join us? We want to be used of God and love Him like never before—and we would love to count you among the growing community of fast friends.

## From Wendy

I won't bother you with which of those jobs listed earlier were mine and which were Suzanne's, but I will tell you that after I quit work to stay home with my children full time, I had a complete identity crisis. I had begun working when I was sixteen and was used to interaction with adults and a paycheck of my own. Now as a full-time stay-at-home mom, I struggled with feeling like a contributing member of society as I folded laundry, changed diapers, and tried to lose the sixty pounds I had gained during pregnancy. By the way, the only one of those three things I actually mastered was changing diapers.

During those early months of domestic and motherhood bliss, I had to fill in various applications for checking accounts, Bible study registrations, and the like. I always got stumped on the "Occupation" blank. I shied away from writing in "domestic goddess," feeling that it was silly and would be discovered to be an outright lie by anyone visiting my home. I was equally uncomfortable with "homemaker" and "housewife." There usually wasn't enough room for filling in the blank with the popular "stay-at-home mom" moniker. "Domestic engineer" sounded a bit pretentious since I am perpetually disorganized and often do my grocery shopping at a convenience store. So

I usually ended up leaving the "Occupation" line blank—until I was reminded of a title I held that was far more regal and exotic than "domestic goddess." Someday I am going to simply put it down on paper. The title that came to me was "princess," or better yet, "daughter of the King."

You see, my sister, that's what each of us is in Christ. We are daughters or princesses of Jesus Christ, the King of kings. Here is a verse worth memorizing in case you ever need to shock yourself out of an identity crisis, as I did:

> The King's daughter is all glorious within;
> Her clothing is interwoven with gold.
> She will be led to the King in embroidered work;
> The virgins, her companions who follow her,
> Will be brought to You.
> They will be led forth with gladness and rejoicing;
> They will enter into the King's palace.
> (Ps. 45:13–15 NASB)

A daughter of the divine King! It doesn't get any better than that. It doesn't matter who you know, who you are, or what you've done. It only matters that Jesus turns pauperettes into princesses and covers us with His beautiful robes of righteousness.

I have been blessed to know Jesus since childhood. I was raised by godly parents and influenced by scores of other fabulous teachers and family members. I have loved Jesus and longed for him since I was a little girl. I have also tested His grace, mercy, lovingkindness, patience, and plan for my life more times than I would ever be able to record. I thank Him daily for the incredible ways He has blessed my life in spite of the many times I have denied Him access, let alone lordship of my life.

I also grew up with girlfriends, my two best being my mother and sister. I had no brothers, so our house resembled more of the antics of Lucy and Ethel in *I Love Lucy* than of Beaver and Wally in *Leave It to Beaver*. My ever-patient father can still be seen shaking his head in disbelief at the females in his house and our harebrained ideas, ability to pick up conversations started and interrupted an hour earlier without missing a beat, and the way we can laugh over just about anything, especially if it is totally unfunny to everyone else at the moment. Girls! Aren't they the best?

As a result of my upbringing, my favorite girlfriends I have met along the way have been the kind with whom you could just as easily share a laugh as a cry. Friends who would love you the same in your sweats and a ponytail as in heels and a suit. Girls who wouldn't cringe at eating a hot fudge sundae after a plate of appetizers and skipping the main meal altogether. Girlfriends who wouldn't mind loaning you a favorite blouse or book because you borrowed theirs last week.

My childhood also placed Jesus above everyone else. My sister and I would tell you the same truth: our mother is the wisest person we know. Since the time we were old enough to grasp the concept, she taught us that Jesus has to be enough. He needed to be our sufficiency and solace. If the Lord provided a husband and friends, that would be a blessing, but they should never take the place of Jesus as our one and only. My mother reinforced that if Jesus is enough, you can joyously embrace life in every moment to live meaningfully, work diligently, pray unfailingly, and laugh unendingly.

So when I met Suzanne, I knew immediately I had a found a friend who also lived this kind of life abandoned to Christ.

In the summer of 2002, my husband introduced Suzanne and me during one of the times of her life and one of the most faith-testing times of mine. She was on the committee commissioned with organizing Franklin Graham's evangelistic outreach for Spokane. I was in the throes of adjusting to the devastating news of our precious little girl's diagnosis of cerebral palsy. Those were trying times.

But have you ever had the experience of difficult circumstances forging an immediate bond with someone in Christ? If so, you will understand what happened to us. We were able to share prayer concerns openly. I can remember sitting at a baseball game with Suzanne early on after meeting her. I broke down in tears as I asked her to pray that my beautiful daughter of twenty months would overcome many of the challenges her cerebral palsy was already causing. We began to communicate regularly over the next few years and exchange prayer requests.

In January 2004, I began to have strange medical symptoms. I would have tingling, numbness, muscle twitches, and many other disturbing sensations. After visiting three doctors, the consensus was the same: I needed to be tested for multiple sclerosis. So, mature Christian that I am, what was my response to such news? Complete panic and hours wasted on the Internet. (By the way, I have learned to avoid researching symptoms.) Although the Lord had told me early on that I did not have MS, I was on the verge of hysteria several times during the weeks following. I let fear grip me and choke out my faith.

Incredibly, unbeknownst to me, Suzanne had been misdiagnosed with MS a few months after the Spokane crusade. Hers was a testimony I needed to hear and prayers I longed to have. She prayed with me continuously and encouraged me to have faith in the perfection of the Lord's plan. Thus began our commitment to fast for a twenty-four-hour period one day a week. We never knew how this practice would change our lives.

For a month I waited to hear from the doctors about my test results. During that time, God taught me many precious things about Himself and my own weakness. Even though He had told me Himself in the still of one night that I did not have MS, and He echoed that message again several more times through His precious Scriptures and prayer, I still doubted Him and panicked, with roots shamefully shallow. The fear that gripped me felt like an outright spiritual attack. My mother and husband would pray with and for me constantly. And all along the way, Suzanne would get on the phone and pray with me as well. Next to my family, there was no one who stood closer to me during those dark days than Suzanne. Thanks be to God for my husband, my wonderful family, and Suzanne! They prayed with me through panic all the way to praise.

For you see, when the doctors finally spoke, God's word to me was confirmed. My MRI and tests did not indicate MS. I had been initially misdiagnosed.

I realize that sometimes the medical news we receive is not good. Sometimes the biopsy is positive. Sometimes the MRI shows MS. Sometimes babies are diagnosed with heartbreaking things like cerebral palsy, as was my beautiful Sydney at fifteen months. Like my mother always taught me, God never promises in His Word that He will tell us the whys. He only promises that He will never forsake us and that He will use all that happens to us for good if we let Him. While there is much I don't know, I do know that God is good and He is in control. This journey of prayer and fasting has reiterated those truths, strengthened my faith, and equipped me to better meet the little trials and huge challenges on this path of life.

## From Suzanne

As Wendy told you, I met her when I worked on a Franklin Graham Festival here in Spokane. I knew right away that we would have a relationship; I just didn't know it would include us becoming fast friends.

Like Wendy, I was brought up in a home of faith, but it was minimal faith. Training in spiritual things was nonexistent, but we did go to church on occasion. I accepted Christ in grade school, but I didn't give him complete control over my life until adulthood. Once I fully surrendered to Jesus, my life was never the same. "Therefore if anyone is in Christ, he is a new creature; the old things passed away; behold, new things have come" (2 Cor. 5:17 NASB). How I ended up working with The Billy Graham Evangelical Association and Franklin Graham is a case in point.

When I first found out that Franklin Graham was coming to town, my prayer was, "Oh, Lord, just let me get involved. Can I sweep the stadium?" Well, being the incredibly big God that He is, He had another plan. I started praying a prayer that was obviously led by God, because the thought did not occur to me prior to exiting my mouth: "Lord, please let me serve you in some way that is media oriented, evangelistic, and bigger than me."

A few nights later, I received a phone call. I thought it was my daughter calling me on my cell phone to see when I would be home. Instead it was the top female news anchor in Spokane. Since I had never met her, I immediately thought the call was a joke, but thankfully the Holy Spirit bound my tongue from saying, "Oh yeah, sure it is!" She asked if I would pray about heading up the media and communications committee for the Franklin Graham Festival. I was speechless—which is a miracle in itself! I said I would pray about it, even though I wanted to jump in and say yes, which is my normal way of doing things.

As I prayed about the opportunity, I realized it was the answer to my prayer; it was media oriented, evangelistic, and certainly bigger than me. I got goose bumps. God moved me to accept the request. The entire experience turned out to be one of the best times of my life. I grew spiritually and began some treasured relationships.

This is just one example among many that have led me to understand that the Holy Spirit shows us what to pray, God answers, and He equips us with His power to do what He calls us to do. And if He leads us through an experience that is heartbreaking instead of breathtaking, He will give us the grace to make it through. This is where the common experience of health issues between my fast friend and me comes into play.

Directly after God had blessed the 2002 festival in Spokane by making it one of the highest-attended North American festivals in the history of Franklin's ministry (more than eighty thousand came to listen to Franklin, and more than four thousand made a decision for Christ), my trials started. The very night the event ended, to be exact. I woke up in the middle of the night, my right eye tearing like a rushing waterfall. All at once, fear attacked me.

I went to the doctor to find out what was going on with my eye. I was told I had an abrasion on my eye for which I would need surgery, that I don't close my eyes entirely when I sleep (which is creepy), and that I needed to put lubricant in my eyes before bed for probably the rest of my life. God got me through this trial, but I soon learned that more was to come. I have come to see that after a spiritual victory, our demonic enemy will try to steal our joy. We have the choice whether or not to allow him to or to believe that God will bring something good and beautiful out of the struggle.

As soon as my eye was healed from surgery, I woke up one morning, walked out to the living room, and suddenly felt the room spinning like a top. I managed to sit down and tell my son to quickly get his dad because something was very wrong with me. I then tried to stand up but ended up on all fours. So it was back to the doctor, and this time the diagnosis was vertigo.

I don't think I have ever experienced anything so debilitating in my life. I could not get to the bathroom without slamming into walls or falling on my face. I could not read or watch the television newscast because I couldn't focus. I couldn't walk, drive, or even begin to take care of myself. The evening when my fifteen-year-old son looked up vertigo on the Internet and told me it could be permanent, I considered revoking his Web surfing privileges until the age of eighteen. I said to him, "Thanks, honey. Mom needed that encouragement. Now excuse me while I go throw up. Oh, wait a minute. I can't walk to the bathroom. Guess I'll just have to do it here." Then I prayed silently, "God, what are you thinking? How can I serve you when I can't even stand up? How will you ever use me in this condition?"

My vertigo life went on for weeks; I felt it would never end. I saw myself as an invalid and a burden to my family. Finally I told the Lord that if this is what my life would continue to be like, I wanted Him to take me home. Knowing my deep despair and the authenticity of it, our gracious Lord prompted my doctor's office to call at that very moment and ask me to come in for a checkup. By the time I got there with the help of my wonderful husband, my vertigo was on the mend, but my doctor suggested an MRI just to be safe. Though I was improving, my symptom of dizziness continued to make me walk for about a month and a half as if I had regularly downed a shot of vodka.

Several days later, when I heard my doctor's voice on the other end of the phone, I got a knot in my stomach. *Why would he call me directly? Is it a bad report about my checkup?* He gave me the news: "I'm so sorry, I didn't expect this, but you have MS." Silence fell on both sides of the receiver. Have you ever had the feeling that time stood still and that you could not comprehend any movement or thought other than being trapped in a moment you wish you could replay but with a different ending? I was dazed. I wanted to say, "This is a joke, right? A very bad joke!" But then the nurse got on the line and prescribed some medication for depression because, according to her, I was *really* going to need it.

Stunned, I told my husband what had just happened. His voice calmed me, and he immediately went into "getting a second opinion" mode. We also made plans to educate ourselves about my "new voyage" in life.

What we learned about MS sent me spiraling into even more shock. Reports of wheel chairs, blindness, and more of the worst scenarios possible were available all over the Internet. I envisioned myself rolling down the aisle at my children's weddings, unable to view the beauty of their being joined with God's choice for their life. Then the quiet whisper of my gentle Savior entered my ear and heart, reminding me that if this was what His plan for me consisted of, He would be in the midst of it, that He who had begun a good work in me would not abandon it. At that point, the floodgates of grace opened up. I began looking at my condition in a new light—a light where I could shine in whatever form my physical being would take, because Jesus had a plan for me.

We waited for eight days to meet with a neurologist for the final sentence. During those eight days, I started to become friendly with my diagnosis. I also appreciated my present state more. The sky was bluer, the trees were greener, and laughter was more boisterous. It was Thanksgiving, and I found that I needed to be thankful—in fact, I wanted to be thankful for things I had taken for granted. I had determined that if God and I were going to travel down this road, He and I would make sure that it counted for something eternal.

The day came when we met with the neurologist. As my husband, Bob, and I performed the niceties of introduction, our hearts were pounding, waiting to hear what the course of treatment would be. As we looked at the MRI with the doctor, we saw strange patches that looked like clouds. Thinking those to be the culprit, you can imagine our surprise when the doctor said, "You don't have MS."

"What? Wait a minute, yes I do," seemed to resonate in my mind. "I have taken almost two weeks to get used to the idea! I've shed many tears, prayed many prayers, and God and I are prepared for this!" But once again shock, only in the reverse. "I don't have MS! I don't have MS! But then, what are those clouds in my brain?" Well, according to the doctor, we don't know what they are. Great, no MS! And yet, no diagnosis either. Just another chance to depend on God in case those cute little clouds are really fluffy ticking time bombs. To this day, no one knows what those strange clouds on the MRI are. But I am thankful that there are no apparent symptoms of a problem either.

So home we went, praising God, getting use to the idea that I had my life back and thanking Him for allowing me to see His grace in action. I can honestly say that I have never felt a peace like that in such a difficult situation. Philippians 4:7 reminds us, "The peace of God, which transcends all understanding, will guard your hearts and your minds in Christ Jesus." He had assured me that He was in control, His plan would be completed, and He would go with me no matter where the path led. God gave me the ability to trust Him on that, and He gave me that incomprehensible peace.

So when Wendy walked the same MS road, I was ready to understand where she was headed. I had been there, and God graciously provided me with the opportunity to pray with her, speak honestly to her, and have my heart beat in sync with hers while we petitioned God to deliver her in the same way He had delivered me.

I know that there are people who have not been delivered from this or many other diseases. I understand only from the standpoint that I have some undetermined issues with my health. I have found that this gives me the opportunity to depend fully on God for my future. It takes me to my knees to pray on a consistent basis for myself and other fellow believers who are suffering. I know whom I've believed, and I know He has a plan. Jeremiah 29:11 says, "'For I know the plans I have for you,' declares the LORD, 'plans to prosper you and not to harm you, plans to give you hope and a future.'" Whatever that plan is for you, dear friends, be in prayer, be faithful, be obedient, and be blessed.

# MOVING AHEAD TOGETHER

So God brought us—Wendy and Suzanne—together. We are sisters in Christ. We pray for and with each other. We fast together. We laugh and cry together. We share our hurts, our joys, our ups and downs. And we do it all knowing that God has created our relationship. We believe He did this, at least in part, because we moved in unison toward Him.

Through our story, we hope you will be encouraged to ask God to help you develop a partnership with a sister in Christ—a partner who will pray with fervor for your requests as you pray for hers. A friend who will intercede when you are too weak or tired to pray anymore for your own burdens. A friend who will gently speak the truth in love when you need to hear it. A friend you can be authentic with and not shy away from dishing the dirt about your own failures and struggles. A friend who won't judge you but instead will pray for you and with you.

We, the authors, are comfortable with each other. Neither of us fears how the other sees us. You know that as women, we can experience feelings of insecurity toward each other, questions of how we will be perceived or accepted. But between us, we can say that we have not experienced even a hint of that. We love each other and accept each other; we root for each other; we laugh and cry in unity.

We don't want you to misunderstand us. We have not been perfect on any level, ever. Just ask our friends or family. But we can tell you that what God has done for us, He can do for you. And that is our prayer for you. We want you to discover through Christ what life can be like with a fast friend.

He is the one waiting for you to seek Him, with the promise that if you seek Him with all your heart, you will find Him. He wants to show you more of who He is and what He can do with the precious life He has given you. He gave His life for us. And He wants to give you a life of immeasurable value.

So let's get started!

# Fast Food for Thought

- ✿ Is God calling you to seek Him in a new and fresh way through prayer and fasting? If you're unsure, go to Him in prayer and ask Him. Then wait for His answer.

- ✿ Will you commit to ask Him to lead you to your fast friend? Pray earnestly over whom God has chosen for you. As He brings individuals to mind, ask Him to narrow down the options to that one person designed to travel this road with you.

- ✿ Once you have a specific person in mind, pray that God will convey to that woman her need to spiritually unite with you. When you get together with this person, listen to her with newly attuned ears, seeking to discern her desire to connect with you as her Fast Friend in Christ.

*Dear Jesus, thank you for bringing us together as friends, support systems, and sisters in Christ. What a blessed bond do those of us have who belong to you, Jesus! We pray for all of those who would like to embark on this Fast-Friend journey. Please bring them their Fast Friend, and let the love and sweet aroma of Christ permeate through everything they are and do, all to the glory of God. Let their lives and legacy be forever changed because of you. In your name we pray, amen.*

CHAPTER 2

# Why Fast?

F asting eventually became an exciting adventure for us, but we want to be honest with you: with two women who love to eat as much as we do, the early days of fasting were an act of sheer obedience. If we hadn't been convinced by the personal reasons that were driving us to fast, we probably would have tried it one time for one meal and called it quits. But we knew that Jesus fasted. So did Moses, Hannah, David, Esther, and the rest of the Jews. Fasting has a lengthy and honored history among God's people. For this reason and others, we felt drawn to this spiritual discipline to strengthen our prayer life. We also looked to fasting to help us with repentance, focus, humbling ourselves, identifying strongholds and breaking them, healing, wisdom, discernment, sacrifice, worship, building our faith, and falling more deeply in love with Jesus. Fasting especially made it easier for us to find more time to pray and to keep "prayer closet" times with God more consistently.

Bottom line, we just knew God was calling us to Himself through fasting and prayer.

Early on, we came across this passage in Ezra: "So we fasted and petitioned our God about this, and he answered our prayer" (Ezra 8:23). That verse got us excited about fasting! What a super simple equation: fasting + petitioning God = answers. Jackpot! We have the formula. *What are we waiting for?* we concluded. So we rushed in, as quickly and excitedly as Peter jumped out of the boat to walk on water to get to Jesus.

We expected that the task would be simple and the solution quickly delivered with minimal effort. We soon learned that this would not be the case. Fasting immediately proved itself a sacrifice. We must relinquish something.

We both remembered growing up hearing friends talk about what they were giving up for Lent. Some would say chocolate, others TV, still others said they would sacrifice drinking sodas. Whatever the choice, the object or activity to give up had to be something important, something of great worth to those making the sacrifice. In the Old Testament, one sacrifice involved the Israelites bringing an animal without defect as an offering in order for it to be acceptable to God. In the New Testament, God sent the perfect Lamb, the One without blemish, to take our place on the cross so that sin could be conquered and we could be reconciled to God through Christ. There has always been sacrifice, and it has always come with a cost.

As individuals, as a church, and as a nation, we are not so enticed by the idea of less. We shop and we buy, we binge and we live in excess, especially here in the good ol' USA.

Why concern ourselves with a budget when we can just pull a piece of plastic out of our wallet and use it to buy whatever we want? We are a people of superabundance. But this abundance of possessions is not what Jesus was referring to in John 10:10 when he said, "I came that they may have life, and have it abundantly" (NASB). The abundance Jesus spoke about was a life in Him that was filled with overflowing forgiveness, love, and grace. This lavish life becomes available to us when we surrender to and believe in Jesus Christ, the one and only Son of God, accepting Him and the sacrifice He made for us on the cross. Notice that abundance comes to us through Jesus' self-giving sacrifice. Since He gave up so much for us, why shouldn't we make sacrifices for Him? When we do, we find out that whatever we give up for Him, we receive in return far more than we sacrifice. We cannot outgive God!

Still, our mentality as a nation and even in some of our churches is that we need to take care of ourselves first. For instance, have you been asked to teach a Sunday school class lately? If so, what was your response? Far too many of us have a reason why we can't or aren't willing to work in our churches. God calls us to something greater than putting ourselves first. He calls us to self-denial and self-control. He calls us to put the needs of others before our own.

Do you want more of Jesus and less of you? Do you want to indulge in Him and less in the stuff you can buy? Do you want to serve Him more than you serve yourself? Do you want to exchange what you can get for yourself for what He can do for and through you? Then the path of prayer and fasting that we are traveling may be the path for you too.

# From Wendy

*Fasting and prayer have taught me to buy less, indulge less, judge less, and say less. And less of me is more of Him!*

The times I have spent fasting have opened my eyes to so many of the ways I had been denying God and indulging myself. I discovered how Wendy-centered I was. One way this became clear to me was in the amount of stuff I had. Come with me through several rooms in my house, and you'll see what I mean.

Let's start with the pantry. In the past I literally had to open one door of the two-sided cupboard and throw things in, shoving the cabinet door closed as quickly as possible so the boxes of cereal didn't come tumbling out. Trying to get out a box of rice or crackers became a risky venture. I won't even bother to tell you about the refrigerator. Way too much food had to be thrown out because it was out of date.

The main rooms of my house are fairly organized because I really don't like clutter. But it's those closets that reveal my true self. Take my hall closet. I call it my "gift closet." It contains the things you buy because you can't pass them up. I would purchase them with the thought that someday I'd hope to find a reason to either use them or give them to someone else. I couldn't go through certain stores without buying things, even if I didn't need them. The closet became so full that I rarely ended up using the "gifts" stuffed in there because I couldn't find them under all the other junk or because I simply forgot about them altogether. Useless accumulation!

Let me take you into my bathroom. Nothing too interesting

here, except for the fact that I owned three scales and would regularly weigh myself on all three throughout the day. Why three? Because I kept buying a new one until I found one that would read accurately, of course! But none of them did. Though I hated what they said, I would step on them again and again in hopes of getting a different reading. I would be amazed that after eating a box of cookies and walking half a block, I hadn't lost weight. I thought, *Why try to put a man on Mars when we can't even make a scale that weighs accurately?* Of course, the scale was right. It was reflecting my unhealthy eating habits.

And yet, I grew comfortable with my size and thought there was nothing wrong with it. Food had become my comforter. Something stressful would happen and I would head to the pantry. I'd eat whatever fell out first. God graciously showed me much about my eating during fasting. He showed me where I ran for comfort, and it usually wasn't to Him. Going without food for a day brought this glaringly to light. The scale wasn't wrong. My heart was and my habits were. Self-denial seemed so foreign to me. I didn't want to believe that I would much rather grab a snack than my Bible. I'd much rather peruse the fridge than the Word.

There's one more place I need to take you. I hope you've had your tetanus shot before we enter. Come with me into my bedroom closet.

One day after fasting, I was convicted about all I had in the way of clothes and shoes. I had clothes in every size from 2 to 12, which represented every size I have been in the previous years. I spent an entire day boxing up and bagging clothes, shoes, and purses—ten huge bags and bins worth. I donated many and threw away more. My closet represented to me the years of overindulgence.

God started to make me feel increasingly uncomfortable with excess in my life. He nudged me gently yet firmly. "Wendy, you have too much, you spend too much, you eat too much, and you say too much. When do you deny yourself for My sake?"

I was completely convicted. The touchiest area where he brought me up short was my mouth. I would feel angry and impatient, and instead of turning to pray, I would speak my mind in whatever way and tone felt best to me at that moment. I would then have to go back to those close to me and have to ask for forgiveness for being unkind and uncaring in my words. I came to know that my heart was involved in this sin, and the Lord really spoke to me about it. I was filling my mouth with food, and I was often using it for my own pleasure and purpose in speaking my mind and revealing my cold heart. Imagine my surprise when I first read the definition of *tsum*, the Hebrew verb for fasting: "to cover one's mouth"! It was as if the Lord was looking me in the eye, saying, "Do you get it? If you do not let My Spirit control you and your mouth, you will continue to live in defeat. Cover your mouth so you can hear Me. Cover your mouth so you will stop sinning against Me. Cover your mouth until My words pierce your heart. Then you can open it. Are you ready to change? Are you ready to feed on My Word? Are you ready to indulge in Me and not in what you desire at any given moment?"

He began to show me how little I denied myself. One Sunday, He spoke to me particularly clearly through a passage of Scripture during a sermon. The text was Hebrews 12:1–4:

Therefore, since we are surrounded by such a great cloud of witnesses, let us throw off everything that hinders and the sin that so easily entangles. And let us run with perseverance the race marked out for us, fixing our eyes on Jesus, the pioneer and perfecter of faith. For the joy set before him he endured the cross, scorning its shame, and sat down at the right hand of the throne of God. Consider him who endured such opposition from sinners, so that you will not grow weary and lose heart. In your struggle against sin, you have not yet resisted to the point of shedding your blood.

The Holy Spirit made some parts of these verses pop out at me. When do I run and strain for Christ in this race of life? When have I tried so hard to defeat sin in my life or deny myself something I wanted (whether it was a material object, a word out of my mouth, or food in my mouth), so much so that it hurt? The only area I could see where I was striving with all my might for something other than myself was for my children's spiritual development. Other than that, I didn't feel like I was running a race for any purpose other than the course I set for myself each day. I was so convicted of this, I cried at seeing myself in this light of absolute spiritual apathy. I didn't live a disciplined life but an indulgent one.

The verses following these in Hebrews are powerful in dealing with the loving and directed discipline of our heavenly Father. The culminating verse on His discipline in our lives is verse 11: " No discipline seems pleasant at the time, but painful. Later on, however, it produces a harvest of righteousness and peace for those who have been trained by it." Fasting is a beautiful discipline. It is one we can participate in with the Father. It is often painful and unpleasant, but the harvest of God's discipline is righteousness and peace.

How about it? Could you use a little peaceful fruit in your life? I certainly craved it. How does the righteousness of Christ sound compared to the self-righteousness many of us feed on and force-feed others? The role I most enjoyed playing in my home was that of the Holy Spirit. I could have had a sign attached to my forehead: "Splinters pointed out and advice freely given. Day or night. No appointment necessary and no need to take notes. Reiteration ad nauseum included in service provided." Or, as it states in Matthew 7:1–5:

> Do not judge, or you too will be judged. For in the same way you judge others, you will be judged, and with the measure you use, it will be measured to you. Why do you look at the speck of sawdust in your brother's eye and pay no attention to the plank in your own eye? How can you say to your brother, "Let me take the speck out of your eye," when all the time there is a plank in your own eye? You hypocrite, first take the plank out of your own eye, and then you will see clearly to remove the speck from your brother's eye.

I knew I had my own planks to deal with, but somehow they didn't seem as offensive as the splinters in others. What would your day be like, family sound like, workplace feel like

… if you lived out the peaceful fruit of righteousness on a daily basis? God challenged me with this during fasting. He confronted me with how little I strove to deny myself so that He could form His living character in my dying self.

By letting God develop me through practicing a Spirit-disciplined life of regular prayer and fasting, He began to achieve His purpose in me. I chose the word *practice* because that is what being disciplined in any way entails. God knows this is not natural to our flesh. He knows that we naturally resist discipline and gravitate toward laziness and indulgence. As soon as we begin to see ourselves through the eyes of our culture, we decide we measure up fairly well. But fasting snaps us out of this realm for a meal, a day, or a lifetime—if we submit to God's discipline.

After indulging in God and fasting from food, miracles in my personality and home happened. The more days I began to fast from food and feed on God, the more He taught me to abstain from many more temptations. I became less angry and impatient. I began not to need to be right and tell others when and how they were wrong. I began to experience his precious and unmatchable peace and see the fruits of his righteousness in my life. This changed for the better my home, my spending habits, my priorities, and so much more.

Interestingly for me, though I began to fast as a way to add depth and fervor to my prayers, I ended up learning my own areas of weakness and need for Him. God knew I began to fast as a desire to see Him answer my prayers more often, and He did honor that. What I didn't realize at the beginning, though, was how fasting would transform my life from desiring to see

Him answer prayers to desiring to know Him and love Him more. I knew it would be hard to go without food. I just didn't know when I began how much I was going to start hungering and thirsting for righteousness. What an awesome, patient, loving, disciplining, demanding, equipping, and empowering God we serve.

## From Suzanne

*Fasting and prayer have taught me to really see the self-imposed excess in my life and see it for what it is—something that needs to be eliminated.*

Sometimes I have to laugh when I read Wendy's story. We have so much in common. I can't resist a bargain when I shop. If it is priced right, I think it must have been made to be mine, and like Wendy said, if I decide I don't need it, I can always use it as a gift. I, too, have been known to eat too much. My cupboards are in disarray because there is far too much in them. It appears I am stocking supplies for the next ice age! As for my closet, well, we had some friends from church over to visit, and their teenage daughter and her friend decided it would be fun to run into our bedroom and sneak a peek at my closet. They ran out laughing and blurted out, "You have too many clothes!" They were right. Even if you peruse the many drawers that are home to my make up, I am pretty certain that I have enough face paint to supply the next Miss America contest—all fifty contestants!

I grew up watching the television sitcom *I Love Lucy*. I remember when Lucy would put a new dress in her closet for a while so that when her husband Ricky saw it for the first time and asked her about it, she could say, "Oh, this old thing? It's been hanging in my closet for a while." My mom also had a strategy with my dad, and it went like this: "Don't you dare tell him I bought this or how much I spent! I will just take it out of my food budget. I'll tell him we're having ham when it's really Spam." Those influences played a big role in my younger life, justifying to me that it was normal to deceive myself about how much I spent or how many things I bought. I reasoned, "If I pay cash for part and pay with a check for the rest, no one will know what it really cost." This approach didn't help me or my husband.

Prayer and fasting helped open my eyes to my deception and the damage sin can cause. God led me to look deep into my heart, listen to Him, and own up to my poor choices. Of course, these poor choices were nothing compared to the ones I had made earlier in life, and maybe that is why I suppressed them. I didn't see them as big sins, just little ones—hardly big enough to matter. What I learned, though, is that there are no lesser sins. Sin is sin. All of it hurts us and others, and all of it offends God. My fasting days brought me needed cleansing from sin. It was as if God gently laid me on His operating table to open me up and meticulously remove my sins one by one.

Through the prophet Isaiah, God revealed His perspective on genuine fasting:

> Is not this the kind of fasting I have chosen:
> to loose the chains of injustice and untie the cords
>     of the yoke,
> to set the oppressed free and break every yoke?
>  Is it not to share your food with the hungry
> and to provide the poor wanderer with shelter—

when you see the naked, to clothe them,
and not to turn away from your own flesh and
    blood?
 Then your light will break forth like the dawn,
and your healing will quickly appear;
then your righteousness will go before you,
and the glory of the LORD will be your rear guard.
 Then you will call, and the LORD will answer;
you will cry for help, and he will say: Here am I.
(Isa. 58:6–9)

Fasting is more than just resisting your hunger. It is an act of service to those in need. It is a lifestyle of being available and having an open-door/open-arms policy to those in your life—your family, your church, those in need in your community, and the other "neighbors" who cross your path.

# WHAT'S AHEAD

*Why fast?* You have heard our answer to this question. We have shared some of what motivated us and how prayer and fasting have impacted us. In the next chapter we will share more of what the Bible says about fasting and prayer, we will answer some questions about these disciplines, and we will talk about some dos and don'ts, especially concerning fasting.

Of course, we encourage you to dig into the Bible yourself to see what it has to say about fasting and prayer. And we certainly hope you will ask God how He wants you to move forward with Him in these precious spiritual disciplines.

# Fast Food for Thought

- Why do you think it would be worthwhile for you to fast and pray?

- What are the biggest fears or obstacles you face in thinking about trying to fast and pray? Are you willing to give God a chance to work through those with you?

- In Isaiah 58, God tells us His perspective on true fasting. If you are not involved in service to those less fortunate than you, consider researching ministries in your area where you can volunteer to feed the hungry, provide clothing for those in need, and be a voice for those treated unjustly. What area can you assist in that resonates with your heart?

*Dear Jesus, as I embark on this journey of fasting and prayer, please empower me, please sustain me, and please fill me with your love, peace, wisdom, and knowledge. Instead of going to food for comfort, I want to find comfort in you. Help me find everything I am and everything I need in you. In your name I pray, amen.*

## CHAPTER 3

# Fasting Matters

*N*ow that you know our reasons for fasting and prayer, we want to share with you some biblical accounts of these activities. We want to encourage you to spend time in the Word and research some of these stories on your own. Allow God to speak to you as you read. Look to Him to guide you to the type of fast He wants you to practice.

*Deuteronomy 9* – Moses fasted for forty days and nights while on the mountain to receive the Ten Commandments from God. For his fast, Moses ate no bread and drank no water. (You should understand that a forty-day fast that includes no consumption of water can only be done through God's miraculous power. Typically, human beings cannot go without any liquid intake for more than a week.)

*2 Samuel 12* – David fasted for the life of his child.

*Ezra 8* – The priest Ezra proclaimed a fast to humble the people before the Lord and ask for a safe journey for all the Israelites and their children.

*Ezra 10* – Ezra fasted from food and water because he was mourning over Israel's unfaithfulness.

*Nehemiah 1* – Nehemiah fasted and wept over the sin of the Jews and prayed that Jerusalem would once again be the center of worship for the God of Israel.

*Esther 4* – Esther asked that all of the Jews join her and her attendants in a fast that involved not eating or drinking for three days and nights. She urged this as preparation for approaching the king to thwart Haman's genocide plan against the Jews.

*Daniel 10* – Daniel's fast was a partial one; he ate only vegetables, grains, and fruits instead of the "choice food … meat or wine" offered to him. He also abstained from lotions. He engaged in these restrictions for three weeks.

*Joel 2* – God instructed the people to fast with weeping and mourning over their sin.

*Matthew 4* – Jesus fasted from food for forty days and nights before Satan tempted Him in the desert.

*Acts 13* – The leaders of the church at Antioch were worshipping and fasting when the Holy Spirit instructed them to set apart Saul and Barnabas for the work to which God had called them.

As you can see, incidents of fasting occur throughout the Bible. And God works through them to accomplish His will.

Notice too that these fasts indicate that God accepts different types of fasts and honors them.

Beyond these passages, you can find many more in God's Word on fasting and prayer. We hope you will do your own search as you seek to understand the truth of this subject.

# Questions and Answers

Along with your Scripture search, you may have some of the same questions we did. Here are the key ones we dealt with. We also give you what we found out along the way.

*We asked:* "We would like to fast, but what if we can't do it?"

*What we learned:* First of all, if you have any health issues, consult your doctor before fasting. If you are healthy enough to fast, you may still experience difficulty. You are not alone in this, for God honors a fast that includes Him. God promises you His power in your struggle: "My grace is sufficient for you, for my power is made perfect in weakness" (2 Cor. 12:9). Let Him carry you.

*We asked:* "What type of fast should we do?"

*What we learned:* The answer to this question is between you and God. Different types of fasts appear in the Bible. Prayerfully seek God for what kind of fasting He wants you to do. Being the creative God that He is, our Father may lead you into a fast that is specific to you. For example, do you spend too much time on Facebook? Let me rephrase that: Do you spend anywhere near the same amount of time in prayer that you do on Facebook? Do you approach prayer with the same excitement you have about reading the most current comments on your Facebook page? Is it easier to text your friends all about your problems than it is to pray? If something that you do takes precedence over Jesus, you may need to fast from it and use the time you would spend doing it to pray. In other words, fasting for you may involve something other than food. Let God show you what fasting for you will look like.

*We asked:* "What if we get hungry? What if we fail to complete the fast?"
*What we learned:* You will get hungry—that's a promise. And if you fall short, God will forgive you and grant you new mercies every morning.

*We asked:* "What will fasting take on our part?"
*What we learned:* It will take sacrifice and determination, even moment-to-moment faithfulness. We know that sounds tough, and in some ways it is. But you will also find that fasting has an upside. Our story alone testifies to how beneficial this discipline has been for us. You will find great benefit too. And what that will be will unveil itself as you move forward with God.

*We asked:* "Will we experience attack from Satan?"
*What we learned:* Most likely, you will, but don't give him too much credit. Consider 1 John 4:4: "You, dear children, are from God and have overcome

them, because the one who is in you is greater than the one who is in the world." The one in the world is Satan.

Prayer is one of the most powerful tools we have to defeat this enemy. He doesn't like it. He will mess with you. But don't chicken out! Remember, Jesus has already won the victory over the devil, and if you put on your spiritual armor, you can deflect all of the arrows your enemy will launch at you (Eph. 6:10–18).

> *We asked:* "Will we really become closer to God? Will we really hear from Him?"
>
> *What we learned:* God has promised that He will answer when we call on Him, and He is faithful. There is an invitation from God in Jeremiah that is a particular favorite of ours. God says, "Call to me and I will answer you and tell you great and unsearchable things you do not know" (Jer. 33:3). The action on our part is to call on God in prayer. God's promise to us is that He will tell us great and unsearchable things we do not know. How can we hesitate, even for a moment, to enter into this kind of intimacy with the Creator of the universe?

He will *tell* us things? Yes, He will, for He is faithful to His Word.

Will you *hear* an audible voice from Him? I don't know. Some people have. We have not. For both of us, God's telling comes to us as a thought that moves through our minds. Perhaps you will hear Him through a song, a sermon, or even a friend's counsel. He definitely uses His Word to speak to us and instruct us. Whatever the means, God will suddenly break through. And in your spirit, you will know He is speaking to you. Just seek Him. He will connect with you.

By the way, when you talk to God, you don't need to be high sounding and super spiritual. Jesus laid out a clear and simple approach for us. He said:

> But when you pray, go into your room, close the door and pray to your Father, who is unseen. Then your Father, who sees what is done in secret, will reward you. And when you pray, do not keep on babbling like pagans, for they think they will be heard because of their many words. Do not be like them, for your Father knows what you need before you ask him. This, then, is how you should pray: "Our Father in heaven, hallowed be your name, your kingdom come, your will be done, on earth as it is in heaven. Give us today our daily bread. And forgive us our debts, as we also have forgiven our debtors. And lead us not into temptation, but deliver us from the evil one." For if you forgive other people when they sin against you, your heavenly Father will also forgive you. (Matt. 6:6–15)

# HOW *NOT* TO FAST (OR HOW TO FAST LIKE A PHARISEE)

Learning what to do is one thing. But sometimes learning what not to do is useful too.

The Pharisees in Jesus' day were the lay leaders of Judaism. They ran the synagogues and taught the Scriptures, which at that time were the books we know as the Old Testament. They also taught the oral traditions that had been handed down through the centuries. These human traditions often undermined what God's Word said, even though they were developed to try to keep people from violating the sacred Word.

To many of the Jews, the Pharisees were the epitome of what it meant to be godly. Jesus, however, saw through the fake outward spiritualized teachings and actions of the Pharisees to the reality underneath. On the matter of fasting, Jesus said this about the Pharisees' approach: "Whenever you fast, do not put on a gloomy face as the hypocrites *do*, for they neglect their appearance so that they will be noticed by men when they are fasting. Truly I say to you, they have their reward in full" (Matt. 6:16 NASB). The "hypocrites" here were the Pharisees and those who emulated them.

Bringing Jesus' observations into our day, Wendy came up with the "Top Ten Ways to Fast Like a Pharisee"—or, to put it another way, how not to fast. We begin with way number ten, counting toward the number-one way not to fast:

10. Complain loudly and frequently about how hungry you are to anyone who'll listen, even if it's to the mailman. If he seems disinterested, make a note to try the paperboy.

9. Sound pathetic and call your husband at work. Ask him to describe in detail what he ate for lunch. Ask frequent questions about the way the

food was prepared and presented if he ate out. Remind him you're fasting, in case he forgot.

8. Watch cooking shows on television and begin planning your meal to break your fast. Start early in the morning so you can consume as many hours as possible thinking about food.

7. Weigh yourself each hour. Consume more time going through your closet. See if your jeans are looser than they were an hour ago. Then think about the outfit you might be able to pull together with those jeans tomorrow! Try on as many options as possible.

6. Spend some time on the computer, make unimportant phone calls, or browse catalogs—anything to keep your mind off that growling tummy.

5. Try to make your children as miserable as you are. Remind them why you are so grumpy, short-tempered, and unable to make cookies with them or dinner for them—*because you are fasting!*

4. If you are at work, make sure to let your boss and coworkers know you are fasting. Use it as an excuse for laziness, exhaustion, sloppy work, and missing that noontime staff meeting. After all, you are fasting and don't need to be around that tempting pizza they order in.

3. Call all of your friends and family the day before to remind them you are fasting and won't be able to join in any get-togethers. Burden them with any of your shirked responsibilities. After all, you've got enough on your (empty) plate.

2. Next, call your Christian friends and the church prayer chain. Alert them to your need for prayer for your fast. Don't bother asking if they have any prayer requests. You will need all your energy to focus on your own needs.

And the number-one way to fast like a Pharisee …

1. Be very proud at the end of your fast. You made it! And if you didn't have any time to spend praying, seeking God, or reading His Word, don't blame yourself! After all, you were fasting. Certainly that will impress God (and everyone else you can think to tell)!

## From Wendy

I am prone to fast as a Pharisee. I came up with the list above fairly easily because I have either done these things or been tempted to do them during days of fasting. *Fasting and prayer have taught me how selfish and petty I can be and how my countenance reflects my heart—for good and for bad.* Here is just one occasion that demonstrates this.

My family wanted to take my grandmother out to celebrate a glowing health report she had just received from her doctor. In fact, finding out she did not have cancer (again) was something Suzanne and I had been praying for. When it was discussed about the best possible time to go out for dinner, the conversation went something like this: "Would six o'clock work for you to have dinner with us?"

"*Well*," I said, "could we go earlier or even the next night, because that is when I am supposed to be fasting."

There was silence on the other end of the phone and a quick pang of conviction in my heart. *What kind of fast does God want, Wendy?* The question resounded within me.

It was inappropriate for me to ask my family to change the time or day of the celebration dinner. Nor was it right for me to make others uncomfortable in my time of fasting. Can you imagine me saying, "Sorry, Grandma. I am really excited for you that you don't have cancer, and I'd *love* to celebrate with you, but wouldn't you know, I can't. You see, I'm fasting that evening. Bummer! But, hey, great news about that negative biopsy!"

Of course, I could have gone to the dinner and ordered a nice glass of ice water and explained to everyone that I was fasting. But this would have turned all attention off of Christ, taken the joy out of my grandmother's time to celebrate God's goodness, and instead focused unnecessary attention on me. Not a proper goal of fasting!

Since I am utterly convinced that God did not command me to fast at a certain time, I was able to quickly readjust the parameters of my fast. I decided to begin an hour later—after the dinner—and extend my fast an hour later the next day. Next, I was able to call Suzanne and tell her about the adjustment of a few hours in my schedule. Did Suzanne care? No. My telling her was simply a way to remain accountable to the commitment we have with each other.

This may seem to you like a rather obvious solution. It is certainly obvious to me now. But I tell you this so you can understand how quickly my mind became legalistic about the parameters of my time to fast. Pharisaic legalism is not dead. I know.

Anyway, on this occasion I was able to joyously and exuberantly eat (not a problem for me!) with Grandma, and go home to my special time with my heavenly Father. He was waiting for me. I knew He would be. His desire in my fast was for my heart, not my legalistic grip on the clock.

God wants your heart and your heartfelt commitment too. He doesn't want you to punch a time clock for some "penitent workday" where five minutes of tardiness will dock your prayer answers by 50 percent. He doesn't give us the gift of a fast to burden us or our loved ones. He gives us the gift of fasting to draw our hearts to Him.

## From Suzanne

It's a scorching sunny day, and I'm headed down the road in my truck. The temperature in my truck is a cozy 93 degrees, and outside it's 100 degrees. I have just polished off the last drop in my water bottle when I realize my thirst is temporarily quenched but my lips are as dry as a desert. So continuing to drive cautiously with one hand, I reach into my bag for my favorite silky, glide-on lip gloss. To my surprise, I instead pull out four chocolate-covered fingers. One of my three precious children must have decided Mom needed a chocolate bar for a treat today. Bless their hearts: they even opened it for me before slipping it into my brand-new handbag! What to do? I have a tissue box on the backseat, but it's out of reach. So, it seems, the only appropriate and natural thing to do is to politely lick my fingers clean. Well, if you can't have lip gloss, delicious to-die-for melted chocolate will do. So in anxious anticipation, my fingers gravitate toward my mouth as my brain screams out the last-minute warning, "You're fasting!"

Well, now wait a minute, let's be reasonable. This is a lick, not even anything that would involve a full-fledged bite. It would just be a little taste, and it smells so good, and it looks so rich and creamy. You have to understand that the women in my family can't resist chocolate; in fact, we have been known to say it is running through our veins. And this chocolate is so melted that it's practically liquid, which would technically qualify as a watery substance. What will it hurt to lick my fingers?

Now you may be thinking that I am being legalistic, but I know me. Once chocolate passes my lips, it is a quick downhill slide. I know I will break my fast and then endure the inevitable self-disgust at my weakness.

"What would Wendy do?" I ask myself. Well, I just happen to know what Wendy would do, because last week on our fasting day, she sat at her favorite Mexican restaurant (Mexican food—another love we have in common), and not one tortilla chip passed her pearly whites. Now that is commitment! There she was at her favorite restaurant with some ministry bigwig, and she didn't eat. But she went to the restaurant because she believed God wanted her to go.

So what should I do? I guess I could pull over to the side of the road and reach for that box of tissue. You see, there is definite blessing in the sacrifice. I know God wants me to fast today. I know He wants me to commit to praying requests that He has big plans to answer. So I pull over, wipe the chocolate off my fingers with a tissue, and whisper a prayer to my precious Savior, who is intimately familiar with the ultimate extent of sacrifice, and I say, "Okay Lord, please help me! I want to do this your way." All at once, the strength to continue the fast and the peace of His presence were more than evident.

Still, there are times when my motives about fasting and prayer go sideways. If you hop on the scale or admire your flatter tummy when passing the mirror, just to see if there has been blessing in the form of weight loss, this is definitely a red flag for misguided motive. Then there is the other end of the spectrum where I look all downcast and devoid of energy. I might as well wear a massive sign that says, "Woe is me, I am fasting!" or "Hey, look at me being all spiritual! Can I get a round of applause for my sacrifice?"

God has been very patient with me, waiting for me to get my act together. One day, however, He spoke to me about my poor fasting attitude. In a much nicer way than I am presenting it, He basically told me to drag my dead weight off the couch, wash my face, make myself presentable to my family, put a smile on my face, and fix my family's meals for the day. I was to be a servant. I was to act as if I wasn't fasting at all. I whispered, "Okay, Lord, but I need you to do it through me, please!" Philippians 4:13 then came to mind: "I can do all this through Him who gives me strength." So I got up and fixed meals throughout the day—and with a smile too. For me, that was a bona fide miracle.

Late in the day, though, temptation arrived when a hunger pang came with a vengeance. Not just desire for food, but a nauseous feeling for lack of it. I came close to nabbing the nachos when a catch in my throat reminded me that some adults, children, and infants, in various places in the world, feel this way every day, and they don't have the option to grab a snack. The nausea quickly turned into a knot in my stomach as I realized how insensitive I was to the issue of poverty and hunger. A torrent of tears fell as I begged God's forgiveness for my lack of self-control and apathy to the suffering of others. My momentary struggle with hunger broke my heart and opened it to others who get to eat little or nothing at all.

*Fasting and prayer have taught me what a wimp I am in regards to sacrifice and how powerful God is in me to provide the self-control I need to persevere. He has softened me to the plight of others, and He has taught me to be truly thankful for the food He has placed on our family table.*

## The Choice Is Yours

So this is where the rubber meets the road. What are you going to do? Are you going to seek a friend who can come alongside you and fast and pray with you? Do you want to use these spiritual disciplines to seek more of God? Do you want to know your Creator and Savior as your first love?

The great patriarchs, priests, prophets, and apostles in biblical times walked with God. They knew Him, heard from Him, sometimes struggled with His will for them, but stayed the course with Him and changed the world. Moses was so close to God that God buried him personally. Deuteronomy 34:6 says, "He buried him in Moab, in the valley opposite Beth Peor, but to this day no one knows where his grave is." Lazarus had such a close friendship with Jesus that our Lord wept at his grave even though Jesus knew He would be raising Lazarus from the dead (John 11:34–35).

What kind of relationship do you want with the Lord? Are you willing to sacrifice to receive something more than you have now?

## FAST FOOD FOR THOUGHT

- ↻ Look up the examples of fasts we mentioned from the Bible. What do these incidents teach you about fasting? About prayer?

- ↻ What questions do you still have about fasting and prayer? What are you willing to do to find the answers you need? What can you do to include God in the process?

- ↻ In what areas are you tempted to fast like a Pharisee, and how do you think you can submit that to God?

🔥 Your attitude reflects what is going on in your heart and your head, just as the outward appearance of those who fast can either reveal their fast or hide it. How do you deal with negative attitudes? Who do you turn to for help in this area?

*Dear Jesus, continue to break my heart with the same things that break your heart. Break me to the point of persistent prayer and aggressive action toward those who suffer daily—the hungry, the fatherless, the widow. As in James 1:27, "Religion that God our Father accepts as pure and faultless is this: to look after orphans and widows in their distress and to keep oneself from being polluted by the world." Motivate me with your love. Thank you for what you have allowed me to learn. Please keep my heart and motives pure. In your name I pray, amen.*

# PART TWO

# Focus Areas for Fasting

"Even now," declares the LORD,
"return to me with all your heart, with fasting
and weeping and mourning."

—JOEL 2:12

## CHAPTER 4

# Fasting
# to Confess Sin

We thank God on a regular basis for the truth of this promise: "If we confess our sins, he is faithful and just and will forgive us our sins and purify us from all unrighteousness" (1 John 1:9). God already knows our sins before we put them before Him: "My eyes are on all their ways; they are not hidden from me, nor is their sin concealed from my eyes" (Jer. 16:17). So if we harbor sin, we only hurt ourselves. What's best for us is to lay our sins before God and ask Him to forgive us. He, in turn, takes those sins away from us. We give Him our worst, and He gives us His best. We can't find a better deal than that!

We have found that prayer and fasting help us see our sins. Sometimes we know what we have done wrong, but too many times we miss what to God is obvious. Prayer and fasting humble us and prepare us to see what He sees about us, to hear what He has to say about us. We have to be honest: learning about the ugliness inside us is hard. But what makes up for it, far beyond the pain and mourning we feel, is God pouring out His forgiveness on us and liberating us as we confess our sins to Him. It's like having the prison doors of our sin thrown open and God telling us to leave our captivity behind and run free! "It is for freedom that Christ has set us free" (Gal. 5:1). Isn't that what you want too?

## From Suzanne

*Fasting and prayer have taught me that sin lurks within me more than I ever realized and the time has come to clean house.*

When fasting comes into view in Scripture, what often comes with it is repentance. God used fasting to bring about confession and restoration with His people. He wanted to purify them by forgiving their sins and welcoming them back into His loving arms.

As I look forward to another day of spending time with the Lord in prayer and fasting, it starts with the realization that I must deal with my *sin*. I really didn't think about sin when I first started this routine with Wendy. All I could think about were the warm fuzzies I would be getting from being close to the Lord, all the amazing answers to our prayers we could look forward to, and how we would grow to become seasoned prayers and fasters. But the reality was, being the loving Father that God is, wanting me, His daughter, to move toward perfection in Christ, He was not going to allow me to go one step further until He addressed the sin issue.

So when I began fasting, God brought a certain conversation to mind that I had engaged in over the phone. I was thrilled when a ministry contact called asking me to help with an outreach event and told me to contact a certain individual to work with. When I contacted this person, he did not want my help. Now you can call it persistence or just plain pesty, but I tried hard to convince him otherwise. After all, someone in a superior position to this person asked me to help with this outreach. So why was this individual trying to prevent my involvement? He was obviously misguided about what we could accomplish together! That thought brought me up short. Did I really think this person wanted to thwart my efforts? I hadn't thought so—until God very gently told me how I had judged this man. I don't think God has a problem with us being persistent, but I do know that He has a problem when we make a judgment like this about someone else. I really believed I was the injured party. I thought I was in the right, that this person made me feel unwanted, unnecessary, and left out. I wasn't happy with him about this, even though I had convinced myself I could be a good martyr and get on with my life. But God's perspective on my conversation unveiled my sin.

God sees those deep, hidden places, where our thoughts are so deceptive that we don't realize we are thinking them until we get quiet before Him in fasting and prayer. I'm talking about the deceptive thoughts that say, "I am doing this for God," but scream out, "They can't do this without me!" … "I didn't ask for this; God sent it my way, didn't He?" … "How come this person is getting in the way and messing it up?" Get the picture?

So when you've suffered what you believe to be rejection, and you go through all the offended emotions thinking you are justified, and you still can't find your way to peace, it's past time to go to God.

On this occasion, I heard the whisper of my gentle Savior say to me about the man I talked to, "You judged him."

I said, "No, I didn't. I just wanted to do what I thought I'd been asked to do, and he wouldn't let me!"

Then God answered, "But you pushed yourself on him and then you judged him. Instead you should have given the matter to me in prayer and left it for me to straighten it out how I wanted."

God was right. I don't think I would have heard Him revealing this to me without prayer and fasting.

I believe that when God calls you to a closer walk with Him and you want Him more than anything else in the world, He also calls you to a stricter place of accountability. Consider what 1 Peter 1:16 says: "Be ye holy; for I am holy" (KJV). He doesn't say, "Try to be holy, will you?" Or, "On a good day, maybe there might be a glimpse of holiness." Have you ever thought about what being holy means? It means to be "set apart." We are not to live as the world does, but to be set apart, true to the gospel of Jesus Christ, and emptying ourselves so Christ can live through us.

If we mean business, we must surrender and become obediently passionate about God, His Word, our walk, our witness, and the love He commands us to live by. I want God to know I am serious enough about Him to take time away from my crazy schedule and food away from my mouth so I can spend some special time traveling with Him on the road to holiness. It's just not possible any other way, at least not for me. I want to be consumed with Him. So does my fast friend, Wendy. How about you?

## From Wendy

*Fasting and prayer have taught me that my sin is ugly and my desire to be right was more important to me than seeing God's righteousness displayed in me.*

It is humbling for me to admit how hard it has been—and still is—for the Lord to break my heart over some of the sin in my life. At different times I have experienced deep hurt, anguish, bitterness, anger, and unforgiveness. When these emotions swirl around in my head and heart without me taking them to the Lord, all thoughts of anyone but myself vanish, and only my wounded heart and pride remain. A "brewing and stewing" pattern creates fertile soil for the enemy to plant seeds of pride and self-sufficiency in me. These are not emotions conducive to a healthy relationship with Christ or others.

God knows our hearts. If you feel unready or unable to let go of a sin, try something that has worked for me. *Ask Him to change your heart!* Confess that you don't *want* to forgive someone, give in on an issue of pride, or stop a practice that is uncharacteristic of His Son. He already knows you feel this way. But then go a step further—ask Him to change your heart. This is what your day of fasting might end up becoming, a time for Him to soften or break your heart so you might have a restored and right relationship with Him.

I have fought for and sought something many times in my

life. It was not glory, fame, or fortune *but to be right*! Can you relate to that? When I have been in conflicts with others or been hurt by someone, part of my flesh cries out for justice and to be right. I have tried for years to play the role of the Holy Spirit in others' lives, neglecting His voice in my own. Isn't there a part in all of us waiting for that moment when someone says, "You were so right in this situation, and I was so wrong. Thank you for pointing out where I was at fault! I really needed to see that. Boy, was I way off base!" Guess what? If this is what you are waiting to hear, you probably will not hear it. Ask yourself, "How many times have *I* gone to someone with words like that?" Your answer will let you know how rare those words are.

While seeking the Lord through prayer, His Word, and fasting, I started to understand that my wanting such an affirmation of my rightness revealed my sin-ridden heart. My demand to be right was actually wrong. My heart was in the wrong place, in the wrong shape. What I needed was a change of heart.

Seeking my Lord for a remade heart has greatly reduced my need to be right. Now I long to see the righteousness of Christ displayed in my life. As stubborn as I can be, the Lord has been faithful and not given up on me. I have experienced what Paul exclaims: "For I am confident of this very thing, that He who began a good work in you will perfect it until the day of Christ Jesus" (Phil. 1:6 NASB).

The key to all of this is that we have to humble our hearts and let Him do His work. Fasting can help us do this, but not automatically. We can fast with unconfessed sin and pride in our hearts, which is a surefire way to fast like a Pharisee. The good news, however, is this: God knows our hearts and loves us anyway! There is nothing we think or harbor even deep within us that catches Him off guard. He desires to fellowship with you and me, to have us know Him and love Him as we never have before.

When we give up something like bitterness, anger, or pride, God wants to fill that newly available space in our heart. He has big plans to give us peace, joy, hope, and encouragement. So seek Him with all your heart. Ask Him to show you something brand new and special, *just for you*, in His Word today. Be amazed at how personal He is and how much He loves you. He has been waiting for years to tell you just how much He adores you. He has been waiting for years to gently form and fashion your willing heart into something beautiful—something He can use to glorify His name. What a privilege and a blessing!

If you have a hard time giving Him your heart, in a step of obedience ask Him to take it and change it for His glory. He has done it time and again for me. He is a gentle surgeon and healer and will bring wholeness to your life. God has already done much to transform me. He has changed me so much that being right really lost its shine. I learned to ask Him not to let me get away with pride and unconfessed sin. He has enabled me to be quick to go to my children, my husband, my friends, and anyone else to ask for forgiveness when I am in the wrong. This is huge. You see, when we give things up, He so often finds a way to even make it fairly painless. It is incredible and quite a secret He shared with me in the dark times. It was as if He was standing in front of a filthy and grubby little girl, saying very patiently, "Are you ready to give that to me, Wendy?" And my reluctant and tight-fisted response was so often, "Well, okaaay," with tears of self-pity streaming down my face as I handed my sin over to Him. Now He simply nudges me with His gentle Spirit, and I gleefully toss that sin right to Him. "Here you go, Lord! I made a mess of that again. Can you please rush your grace, mercy, and redemption in to cover that?" I am deeply thankful for the journey He has taken me on and so amazed that it took me so long to get here.

## HIDDEN MOTIVES AND ATTITUDES

Sin can be outward or inward, obvious or hidden. We have found that frequently the harder sins to deal with are the hidden ones, especially when they involve our motives and attitudes.

When you begin to seek God and ask Him to reveal your hidden motives and attitudes, it can be a wonderful yet painful teaching time. When you realize what you have been doing is wrong, it grieves you. When you realize you have been doing it in front of other people, it can be humiliating and embarrassing. And unfortunately, if it has been an attitude you displayed in public, it is something you cannot erase. Worse yet is if someone caught you on video and the scene made it to YouTube! Thankfully, we have a good, gentle, loving heavenly Father who speaks to us in tones that correct and encourage. He never seeks to condemn us.

# *From Suzanne*

*Fasting and prayer have taught me to ask myself before I speak out loud, "What do I want to accomplish by saying that?" I am shocked by how often my motive is wrong, unedifying, or would inappropriately reveal someone else's wrongdoing. I then have the choice to take the narrow road or the wide one. Fasting and prayer have made motive and attitude checking a regular practice for me.*

We are told in Scripture to guard our hearts: "Above all else, guard your heart, for everything you do flows from it" (Prov. 4:23). We cannot guard our hearts without paying attention to our motives and attitudes.

Has anyone ever come to you with a prayer request that has attitude with it? The kind that says, "I really care about this person and want you to pray for them"? The words sound fine, but as the person tells you more about what she wants you to pray for, you begin to realize that the underlying motive is, "I really want to tell you what this person is doing or going through because it's kinda juicy, and then maybe it will elevate me in your eyes because I would never do anything like that!" Or how many times have you or another sister in Christ confided in someone about what another person did to wrong you? And yet Scripture clearly states that we should go first to the person involved, not to someone else: "If your brother or sister sins, go and point out their fault, just between the two of you. If they listen to you, you have won them over" (Matt. 18:15). Maybe you tell yourself that you need to talk to someone about this person because if you went to her, you just know she would not receive it in the right spirit. Have you considered, though, that you could fast and pray over the situation before you go to her, asking the Lord to bless your efforts and restore your relationship? Or maybe you haven't done this because you really don't love that other person as God has told you to and you are being driven by an ulterior motive? I understand that sometimes we need wise advice. But too often this rationale may hide what we are really doing, which is gathering allies for our side of the story and gossiping about the other person. We need to take heed that "A perverse person stirs up conflict, and a gossip separates close friends" (Prov. 16:28).

Here's another scenario that often plays out. We have all most likely felt anger and a desire for setting the record straight when someone hurts us, one of our children, or someone we love. On the outside, we may not say that we wish the wrongdoer harm; after all, that would not be Christlike. But then comes the day when that person encounters some difficulty. This is when somewhere deep in the recesses of our deceitful heart, a slight hidden smile appears. We are secretly pleased that the one who did the wrong got their just desserts.

I found out that God dislikes this attitude. Proverbs 24:17–18 says, "Do not gloat when your enemy falls; when they stumble, do not let your heart rejoice, or the Lord will see and disapprove and turn his wrath away from them." I had not read this passage until recently. When I did, it struck home. You see, there was a time when I used to hear a soft "Yippee" in my mind when someone got what I believed was justice. But then I had to ask myself, "Who made me judge?" Absolutely no one! God in His mercy has transformed me. I know I am to restrain from judgment and instead love others and pray for them to be blessed. As Paul says in Romans, "Bless those who persecute you; bless and do not curse" (Rom. 12:14).

Sometimes we don't realize what we are doing and why until it has caused irreparable damage. I am so thankful that our God searches the intent of our heart and brings what is hidden to light so we can face the situation, confess what we did wrong, and seek reconciliation as far as it depends on us (Rom. 12:18).

A powerful hindrance to the approach God desires is pride. I know this firsthand. He has been dealing with the deep, hidden pride of my heart. I'm going to refer to it as the *P* word. It hinders us from a pure heart that has pure motives and attitudes. Here's what God says about the *P* word: "The LORD detests all the proud of heart. Be sure of this: They will not go unpunished" (Prov. 16:5). Pride is opposed to God and what He prizes. But spotting it and rooting it out are not easy.

My bouts with pride began a few years ago, but I didn't hear God about them until I fasted. I've gone through three stages over these years.

## Stage P-1

Initially I felt really open about sharing with everyone God's revelation to me about serving Him full time as a volunteer in any ministry He chose for me. At first it was because I was excited about hearing from the Lord. I wanted to tell others how God had answered my prayer and testify to His goodness.

But soon I caught myself saying things like, "Boy, once you let people know you are in full-time ministry and will work for free, opportunities come out of the woodwork!" Then, there was my comment: "I am so busy, but I guess if I'm going to place myself on the altar, I shouldn't tell God how high to turn up the heat!" Then I threw myself a pity party to accompany my pride, which I only expressed to myself, thankfully: "Woe is me, look at all the people doing ministry and getting paid for it, but I have been chosen to sacrifice." Now the last two sentences were so sly that I did not even acknowledge them until the Lord broke through and made me listen to myself. My response was the desire to hide and cover my ears from the embarrassment of my huge lack of humility and misguided motives. But once again, my heavenly Father called me into His presence and gently urged me to confess, repent, and be graciously forgiven.

## Stage P-2

Then came a wonderful event that I just knew God wanted me to get involved with. However, I was already overbooked. Still, convinced God wanted me to do this, I "obediently" added it to my plate and then asked the Lord how in the world this would all work out. Did you notice the wrong order of events here? I should have asked God *before* I said yes to the new opportunity. So God, in His wisdom, used my foolish decision to refine me and help someone else. He told me, "I have chosen an assistant for you." Then He wanted me to present the opportunity to her. That sounded great to me. So I called this woman, and she told me that she had been praying and asking

God to let her serve Him by getting involved with this particular event. Confirmation! Yeah!

Now this event involved public relations for a large evangelical gathering. Since I have experience in this area, I assumed I could handle all the big stuff, and my assistant could handle all the paperwork. All of a sudden and to my surprise, God started giving her some great ideas—ideas that had never crossed my mind. So she obeyed Him and moved ahead.

This ruffled my feathers! "God, this was supposed to be my area of authority," I complained. "What's going on here?" Then, subconsciously, I began wanting to keep her at bay. This is where that subtle sin comes in, the one that automatically pops out when there is still too much *self*. "Maybe I should take some meetings without her; it really isn't necessary for her to be there," I reasoned. "I will let her be at the ones that I choose for her to attend. She can help when I decide she can help."

Then, one night, God woke me out of a peaceful sleep. I awoke to the voice of my Father saying, "I have chosen her." You know what my first thought was? *You didn't choose me; You chose her!* Suddenly I was filled with insecurity and the recognition that I had sinned.

God had deemed it important enough to wake me up to straighten me out about His plans for another of His daughters. I eventually fell back asleep, only to rise in the morning and become immediately aware of my middle-of-the-night revelation.

Instead of praying about this, I quickly jumped to the conclusion that God must not have picked me but her for this job. This is not the way to handle things, girls. I should have gone to prayer right away and asked God to forgive me and give me clarity. Instead, several hours of agony later, I finally fell on my face before the Lord in tears. He then sweetly whispered in my ear that He had chosen me to train this woman. She was to learn what I had learned at His feet and by His grace. He was giving me the privilege of mentoring her, and I was not to hinder her growth in any way. God led me to be in prayer for my sister in Christ—to nurture her, encourage her, love her, and give her the opportunity to learn. With that, my selfish, want-it-all-for-myself feelings went away.

## Stage P-3

When I attended my church one Sunday morning, I witnessed one of the most wonderful dramas I have ever seen at our church. It was a near-perfect script, near-perfect casting, and almost-perfect acting. And as several people approached me afterward to tell me what a good job I did, I had to say, "Oh, well, that one wasn't mine." See, for the previous year, I had written (in the Lord's power) almost every single script presented in our Sunday services. And once again, I had subconsciously acquired a taste for ownership of these presentations. God decided that day, however, that He was going to set the record straight inside my head and heart about who owned what.

Growth through P-2 had taught me to share in the victory of others in the body of Christ rather than be selfish and try to reign over my particular area of gifting. God gently spoke to my heart on this occasion, and here are the instructions I heard for dealing with wrong reactions in the area of pride:

- Rejoice in whatever victory God brings through any part of His body.
- Do not take ownership of God's work, but be committed to do your very best to serve Him when He does call on you. Do not hold tightly to anything, for everything belongs to Him.

- Do not be prideful, but boast in the Lord. Encourage others who have a similar gifting to yours. Work together to serve Christ.

First Corinthians 12 tells us that all Christians are members of the one body of Christ, and some of us have similar gifts, some very different ones. But just as a human body has eyes, ears, limbs, and so on, we Christians have specific talents and purposes in the church body that make us complete in Him and in ministry. And all of our giftedness comes from the same Lord: "Now there are varieties of gifts, but the same Spirit. And there are varieties of ministries, and the same Lord. There are varieties of effects, but the same God who works all things in *all* persons" (1 Cor. 12:4–6 NASB).

Just because another part of the body uses their similar gifting doesn't mean that God won't use me too. The ability and equipping given us is always from the Lord. The finished work and its result are God's, not mine. The entire body of Christ must rely on God in order to fulfill His will. It is sin to ever take praise or responsibility for what God alone can do. And it is by faith in our loving God and Savior that anything of worth is accomplished.

# Moving Through Our Failures

Jesus said, "Simon, Simon, behold, Satan has demanded permission to sift you like wheat; but I have prayed for you, that your faith may not fail; and you, when once you have turned again, strengthen your brothers" (Luke 22:31–32 NASB).

## From Wendy

*Fasting and prayer have taught me that when I fail, Jesus has already seen it coming and has a plan to use it. I have also learned that if I can stop quenching the Spirit, I can have fewer failures.*

One thing that brings me more peace than almost anything else is knowing that God has foreseen my every failure and loves me anyway. I never shock Him with my poor choice, rebellious behavior, or stubborn heart. I often shock myself but never Him. I often hate myself for my failures, but He never does. And it is this love and grace that changes our failures into strength-building exercises—for our good and His glory. When the jars of clay get broken, His light can finally get into the deepest and most desperate parts of who we are.

I am so thankful that Jesus told Peter that He knew Peter was going to blow it. Because of this, Jesus prayed for two specific things: that Peter's faith would not fail, and that he would repent and use his experience to strengthen his fellow believers.

This is our God. The Son intercedes at the right hand of

the Father for us, praying for our faith and ministry, all the while knowing that we will experience failure. What better or more faithful prayer partner could we want? He knows when we are about to make a huge mistake—when we are about to say the thing, do the thing, post the thing, reveal the thing that we are going to deeply regret but are too silly or stubborn to see. First, the Spirit tries to stop us. But when we quench Him, the deed is done and the consequences are headed our way. Yet, the story doesn't end there for those of us in Christ. He will take that ugly, awful failure and use it for the good of those who love Him. Unbelievable! If we could grasp the magnitude of this, we would not live in shame, wallowing in our guilt. We would live in humble and amazed excitement to see how He is going to cover, bless, and use our weakest moments for His kingdom purpose.

As women, we often feel defeated by our failures. My most anguished nights have been spent in some sort of pain and pleading with the Lord over ways I have blown it. If you are a mother of any age, you know the mommy guilt you carry. We later discuss fasting and praying for our kids, but I know that any mother (and father too!) has felt a deep horror at some awful mistake she made, did, or said regarding her kids. Or how about the nights you have laid awake wishing you could take back that careless comment at work? Or what about the secret you passed along before you remembered you weren't supposed to tell?

Through the years of fasting and praying, I have been set free from the horrible weight of my failures. I am now able to give them to God right away and ask for His help and intervention. There are many nights when I blew it with my words that I have prayed, "Lord, please take that away from Sydney's mind and heart." The Lord has taught me through seeking Him in these moments that He is the Redeemer. If I ask Him to rush in, save me, and redeem the situation, His Spirit comes pouring in and restores my soul. Then I am able to hear what I am supposed to say or do next to make amends. If it is out of my control to do anything about the failure, then I have learned to simply leave it in God's hands and pray for His will to be done.

One reason we fail is that we quench the work of the Holy Spirit in our lives. Rather than giving Him full reign, we hold back from Him—rather than submit to Him, we do our own thing. But if we stop quenching the Spirit, we will actually make fewer mistakes.

Here are some signs that, if present in your life, may indicate that you are quenching God's Spirit.

- Your Bible has dust on it.
- If you are reading your Bible, you are getting nothing out of it.
- No one has asked you to pray for anything in a long time.
- In fact, you haven't prayed for anything in a long time.
- When you go to church, you spend more time focusing on what others are wearing than on what is being sung about or shared.
- Your children have started wishing out loud for "Happy Mommy" to come back.

- You have "consumption" from the amount of food or purchases you have been consuming.
- You feel a little grudging toward putting that love gift in the mail for an outreach you have pledged to support.
- You really would rather sit in your room and mope rather than face the responsibilities of the day.
- You haven't felt convicted of sin in a long while. In fact, you are downright bothered by the sin of others at the moment.

If you can relate to the list at all, let me make you feel better by saying how many seasons of my life I cycled in and out of these quenching moments. I am serious when I say my daughter would wander around and wish for "Happy Mommy" to come back because I was so grouchy and impatient all the time. If you are quenching the Spirit, you will know it in some way or another.

One biblical point of reference is to gauge yourself by the deeds of the flesh or the fruit of the Spirit listed in Galatians 5. Paul tells us that "the deeds of the flesh are evident … immorality, impurity, sensuality, idolatry, sorcery, enmities, strife, jealousy, outbursts of anger, disputes, dissensions, factions, envying, drunkenness, carousing, and things like these" (vv. 19–21 NASB). In other words, whether you are obsessively consumed with social media or making tennis an idol of your time; whether you are having an affair or envying your friend's new Chanel bag; whether you drink too much too often or have frequent outbursts of anger at your children, husband, or employees … you are exuding the flesh. The examples are endless, but you get the idea. It was always the outbursts of anger that would convict me and reveal to me that I was quenching His beautiful, precious, peaceable Spirit.

Compare the deeds of the flesh with the fruit of the Spirit, which consists of "love, joy, peace, patience, kindness, goodness, faithfulness, gentleness, self-control; against such things there is no law. Now those who belong to Christ Jesus have crucified the flesh with its passions and desires. If we live by the Spirit, let us also walk by the Spirit" (Gal. 5:22–25 NASB).

In which world would you rather live—the world of the flesh or the world of the Spirit? Which fragrance would you rather wear? Which nature would you rather quench—your own or God's? It takes practice to abide in His Spirit and the Word His Spirit has inspired for our instruction. But the more you practice submitting to Him rather than to yourself, the more you will evidence His fruit, both within yourself and without. Through your times of prayer and fasting, ask the Lord for more of His Spirit. It is a request He loves to fulfill.

## WHERE GRACE ABOUNDS

Don't let your sins—whether they are bad choices, pride, a lapse in seeking the Lord, wrongful motives, or anything else that hinders your growth in Christ—define you for even a moment. All you need to do is confess those sins and turn away from them, and then God's grace will pour out like a fountain.

One more thought. Take comfort in the fact that when you confess your sins, they are gone. Removed as far as the east is from the west (Ps. 103:12), cast into the depths of the sea (Micah 7:19). Knowing God has buried your sins in the deep, don't go deep-sea fishing after them. Leave them be. If guilt over those nasty, sea-soaked sins seeps back into your life, simply thank God again for removing those sins from you. Even if you have to do this a thousand times, resist the temptation to keep fishing those hideous sins back up. Our enemy wants us to fail and remain enslaved to our sins. But God wants us free from them and to find our ultimate fulfillment in Him. Rest in Him. Let His Spirit do His work in you. Eventually, the enemy will get bored reminding you of your sin when you are constantly praising God for forgiving you.

# Fast Food for Thought

- ✤ What areas of unconfessed or unforgiven sin are hindering your freedom? Will you take those to God today?

- ✤ Have you begun to acknowledge that there could be some impure motives or attitudes that drive your actions? Are you willing to let God bring those to light and remove them?

- ✤ Do you inquire of the Lord prior to accepting a "great" opportunity, to insure He has chosen you for a specific position or role? If your answer is no, is it because you are assuming ownership of something that is God's?

🍂 How might you be quenching the Spirit? Will you commit to pray about this and see what He shows you?

*Dear Jesus, thank you for your sacrifice of dying on the cross for our sins. Thank you for the love that drove you to suffer unimaginable pain, rejection, and disloyalty so that we could live. Thank you that you want us to bring our sins to you in repentance, not so you can condemn us or punish us, but so you can set us free. Thank you that you invite us to bring our sins to you: "Though your sins are like scarlet, they shall be as white as snow; though they are red as crimson, they shall be like wool" (Isa. 1:18). You paid the price, you conquered death, and we have reaped the eternal benefits. As it says in the Lord's Prayer, forgive us our sins as we forgive those who sin against us (Matt. 6:12). Please show me areas of sin I need to confess to you or forgive in someone else. In your name I pray, amen.*

## CHAPTER 5

# Fasting for God's Guidance

J esus told us, "Ask, and it will be given to you; seek, and you will find; knock, and it will be opened to you. For everyone who asks receives, and he who seeks finds, and to him who knocks it will be opened" (Matt. 7:7–8 NASB).

God freely invites us to seek Him through prayer and find guidance and counseling through His Holy Spirit. His Word is our guidebook for life. However, there are times that we don't consult Scripture, pray, or listen to the Spirit. When we don't, we forfeit learning His guidance and are left to figure things out using our own resources. We would all do well to remember Proverbs 2:6: " For the Lord gives wisdom; from his mouth come knowledge and understanding."

## From Suzanne

*Fasting and prayer have taught me to go to the Lord with the big and the small, even with what seems silly. I seek Him, listen for Him, and watch for what He will do. I have learned that He gives wisdom freely, but I did not realize prior to fasting how much I wanted His counsel. Now I understand its unsurpassable value, and I believe without wavering that I will receive what I ask from the Lord.*

There was a time when my kids were getting a little more self-sufficient, and I felt God leading me to add to my schedule something outside our home. I was certain that I had heard from the Lord about pursuing ministry instead of getting a job or going back to school. Then one day, my husband suggested that I do *volunteer* ministry because he was doing well enough to support us. I thought this might be the answer to my deep desire.

God's first revelation of His plans for me was a bit difficult to comprehend. About this time, a good friend of mine approached me and said she had heard something from the Lord for me. She told me that God had revealed to her that He was going to have me serve Him in the field of faith-based entertainment. This seemed far-fetched to me. I lived in little ol' Spokane, Washington—not exactly the central hub of the entertainment industry. Unless God was planning an earthquake that would uproot Hollywood and drop it smack dab in the middle of our quiet little burg, I didn't see how what my friend said was even remotely possible.

Nevertheless, I did pursue some minor public relations situations that came up. Different faith-based events needed someone to get the word out creatively. So I jumped from event to event, doing what the Lord instructed me to do. This was back in the day when I started to hear from the Lord about fasting and Wendy called with the invitation to join with her.

God had been working on both of our hearts at the same time.

I did not consult the Lord and decided to put prayer and fasting on hold for the summer to freely enjoy my children. In late August, we went as a family to our local theme park, Silverwood. We found that the park had constructed a climbing wall. Now I had climbed one before, quite successfully. My husband and boys were not present when I did my climbing, so I figured this was a great chance to prove to them that Mom still had it. I got harnessed in and started my timed climb. Well, to my surprise, I couldn't even get halfway up without miserably failing. This was more than embarrassing. I felt as if my legs were noodles. I had no strength and no coordination. Ugh! I quickly gave up, only to hear one of my boys say, "Why did you quit?"

Of course, I could have prayed and asked the Lord for help, but I had put that on the back burner for the summer. Even before the climb, I could have asked the Lord to help me, but I forgot about Him temporarily because I was set on showing off.

Soon, September came and school was back in session. Now that it was convenient and I had more time, I started to fast and pray again. I began seeking Him again about serving Him full time strictly as a volunteer in whatever ministry He chose for me. I asked Him to give me a very specific answer—one I could point back to in the future. So He gave me Job 31:4, "Does he not see my ways and count my every step?"

Now it was the second week of school and time for sixth-grade camp. I had never been before because my husband, Bob, had always gone with the boys. But this time my daughter was going, so it was my turn too.

On the day we left for camp, Bob strongly recommended that I try the ropes course there. I said I would check it out.

Well, the second afternoon at camp, fear set in as I was introduced to the ropes course. The course was a cable thirty feet in the air with suspended short ropes above it, ready for us to maneuver it as if we were tightrope artists. Most of the kids couldn't wait for the camp representative to harness them and send them up a twenty-foot ladder and then another ten feet up a pole that had little hooks in it for climbing. Once the kids got up there and placed their feet on the cable, many of them looked like they probably should have visited the bathroom just before the climb.

So my precious Nicki said to me, "Mom, you have to do this!"

"Yeah right, honey," I replied, feeling the horror of Silverwood all over again, only magnified about a thousand times. *This is what Bob was referring to?* I thought. "How could he possibly suggest this after my last attempt at climbing?" When I mentally compared the wall at Silverwood to this ropes course at camp, I felt as if Silverwood's wall was like the hill in our front yard while the ropes course might as well be Mt. Everest! Looking at the excitement in Nicki's eyes, something told me that I was not getting out of this challenge.

Well, I harnessed up and stood by the ladder. Before the ascent, each of us had to announce our names to the whole group and say, "I accept this challenge!" When it was my turn, the words that came out of my mouth were, "I'm Suzanne, and I don't think I'm ready for this!" But there was no turning back.

As I made my first move up the ladder, I prayed, "Lord, if

you help me do this, with no fear, and I actually succeed and enjoy it, I will take this as my sign that I am to do ministry full time, committing to it as a volunteer and serving in any role you choose. Please reveal your will to me." I knew He would be faithful, based on 1 John 5:14–15, which says, "This is the confidence we have in approaching God: that if we ask anything according to his will, he hears us. And if we know that he hears us—whatever we ask—we know that we have what we asked of him." I had no premeditated plans of uttering that prayer; it just slipped out.

But after I prayed it, I knew it was the leading of the Holy Spirit. (I am accustomed to God catching me off guard to get my attention since my mind tends to be very active.) So trying to forget my failure at Silverwood, I started to climb, becoming increasingly aware that I was really intent on the process and felt perfectly calm.

When I reached the cable, my first step onto it was actually void of fear. I walked along the cable, reaching for the hanging ropes above me without any hesitation. I had a blast and experienced nothing like the Silverwood fiasco. When I was finished, one of the parents who had been watching said, "You did great! You never looked the least bit nervous!" I knew that God had given me my something to point back to.

God's answer to me was unforgettable. Thinking back to my earlier climbing failure, I knew that God allowed this second experience to remind me that when I attempt even small things on my own, I risk failure. But with God's power and my willingness to submit to Him, any cable, climbing wall, or ministry attempts have purpose and will be successful. So that night I slept well, knowing that God had answered my prayer. Now I would listen for where He would lead me in ministry.

The next camp day, we started out on a rainy hike up a mountain. I debated over whether to go, but felt the nudge of the Holy Spirit to take the trek. Halfway up the hill, I stopped to look at the lake, the trees, and the sky and was astounded by the beauty of God's creation. At that moment I heard God say, "If I took this much care creating and forming this beautiful sight, which is not eternal, just think how much more care I will take in forming, preparing, and directing you, my precious eternal child, for my service!" Philippians 1:6 resounded in mind: "Being confident of this, that he who began a good work in you will carry it on to completion until the day of Christ Jesus." I claimed that truth. To this day I still get chills when I remember God's word to me on that hike.

I went home on a cloud, praising God and listening intently for His leading. I was incredibly thankful that God had provided Bob with the kind of job that could support our family of five. Even with college facing us in one short year for our son Tyler, I knew I didn't need to be concerned about helping out financially. So Wendy and I continued to pray and study together, focusing on Hebrews 11 and Romans 4.

There we read accounts of believers such as Abraham, Noah, Moses, and Rahab. They all trusted God, even when life looked desperately hopeless. Having a desire to please the Lord, I memorized Hebrews 11:6: "And without faith it is impossible to please God, because anyone who comes to him must believe that he exists and that he rewards those who earnestly seek him." I continued on in my prayers and pursuit of great faith, all the while not knowing that I was in preparation for an imminent shock.

Bob had told me that some changes might be coming at his work with the introduction of new management. That leadership change led to a drastic reduction in my husband's paycheck. How could I now pursue full-time volunteer ministry when our cash flow was so diminished?

I checked in my spirit to see if God might be chastising us. I came to believe that this was not the case, that God was allowing this financial change for our good. It would certainly prove to be quite the faith-building exercise. My initial thought was, "Well, I will just have to go back to work." I started planning what to do as I degraded myself for not finishing my college education and thereby lowering my ability to find a job with the income we needed.

In the midst of my attempts to solve our financial problem, God's voice broke in. He spoke to me something like this:

*God:* "What about my plans for you? What about serving me in volunteer ministry?"

*Me:* "But you have to understand, that has changed now."

*God:* "No, it hasn't. I have a plan, and I gave you a vivid answer to your prayer to me. Stay on course and you will succeed, just like you did on the ropes course."

God, by His grace, replaced my panic with His peace. Soon I began quietly anticipating what He would do next. He knew that the ministries He allowed me to volunteer with would become centers for my education—an education that would position me to work in faith-based media, which twelve years later is where I currently serve Him. For that very reason, I needed to remain a volunteer. God launched me into my own individualized "ropes course." My choice was to either trust and obey or worry and be dismayed. Jesus helped me choose the trust and obey option.

Prior to Bob's employment difficulties, we had prepaid a trip to California to spend Thanksgiving with Bob's family. Bob told me to rent a van for our arrival, fully realizing that it wasn't really in the budget. That night, someone who knew about our upcoming vacation called (unsolicited) and offered us their large car for the week. The van rental was now unnecessary. This was only the beginning of God showing us how He would provide for us. Paul tells us, "my God will meet all your needs according to the riches of his glory in Christ Jesus" (Phil. 4:19). And that is what the Lord did for us and is still accomplishing in our lives.

I am slowly beginning to realize that it is an honor to have the Creator recognize our needs and offer to take care of them for us. I needed to repent of my lack of faith and the stress I carried over our financial issues. I also needed to begin to praise God in all things and thank Him in advance for what He would supply. Once again, my life verse popped in my head: "'For I know the plans I have for you,' declares the Lord, 'plans to prosper you and not to harm you, plans to give you hope and a future. Then you will call upon me and come and pray to me, and I will listen to you. You will seek me and find me when you seek me with all your heart'" (Jer. 29:11–13).

# From Wendy

*Fasting and prayer have taught me to love God's Word and to feel His voice come alive. They have helped me know the path to choose and to trust the way He leads.*

I am a horrible decision maker. I don't mean that I necessarily make bad decisions; it's just that there are so many options, and I like to weigh them all. I can't pick a tree at the Christmas tree lot. I have trouble choosing a nail polish for a pedicure. I have to hear what everyone else is ordering before I am sure what I want to eat. And the list goes on. My family is patient with me, usually, and while caution is a good thing, indecision is not. Maybe you can relate.

What's funny is that I now have a career where many people depend on my ability to help them make decisions. Big decisions that affect their finances and families for years to come. It is a weighty responsibility, and one I take seriously.

In the years I have been fasting, praying, and diligently seeking God, He has brought me to a place where I am finally able to ask for His help and be certain I am receiving it. Talk about a life changer! For years, I would have to call my five closest friends, my mother, and my husband to make decisions on things like where the kids should go to preschool or what sounded good for dinner. It was partly because I am relational, and mostly because I was reluctant to make a bad decision. Terrified of it. God began to deal with me about this and show me how I often came to Him as my last resource for advice. I had gotten in the habit of seeking godly counsel before I would actually seek God, and it often left me confused and frustrated. Especially when my go-to sources had differing opinions.

I began to feel led to fast *from* seeking guidance help outside of God and His Word. I told myself I would seek Him first and go to others for confirmation of what I felt led to do. This was a leap of faith for me. I took to heart James 1:6–8: "But if any of you lacks wisdom, let him ask of God, who gives to all generously and without reproach, and it will be given to him. But he must ask in faith without any doubting, for the one who doubts is like the surf of the sea, driven and tossed by the wind. For that man ought not to expect that he will receive anything from the Lord, being a double-minded man, unstable in all his ways" (NASB). What a challenge this was for me—and what a promise! I could ask for wisdom, and God would give it generously. The only condition would be my faith and refraining from doubt. I decided to give God and His wisdom a try.

I think this is a huge challenge in our generation. Even as Christians, we are tempted to find wisdom in all sorts of places. Some of these are great and useful tools. My ninety-two-year-old grandmother loves Dr. Oz, for example. Some people will hop on the Internet and search home remedies or consumer reports before deciding a treatment or the best vacuum to buy. There is a lot of information out there in this age of information. And much of it is a gift in so many ways. But, maybe God and the Bible have scooted down on the list of resources that come to mind when we need help with seeking wisdom. Information can be true or false, good or bad, wise or foolish. Instead of spending so much time searching through the mountain of information in order to find some nuggets of gold, I suggest that we fast and pray for self-discipline to seek God and His wisdom first. The flesh is too quickly drawn to the easy, broad information highway. The spiritual path is the better one to travel.

Knowing this, however, does not always translate into acting on it. For instance, just recently my family was presented with the option to change states for my husband's job. Rather than turn to God, I immediately got caught up in looking at real estate in the new city and checking out schools, the shopping (don't judge), even churches and weather as I was contemplating the pros and cons of relocating. None of this activity was wrong. In fact, there is some wisdom in this, and God expects us to use our minds and experience in making life decisions. However, the problem was that I hadn't sought God's view first—in fact, not at all. I just started wasting hours of time wrapping myself up in information to the point of distraction. I had not put any concerted effort into praying about this opportunity and challenge. I was already planning on the timing of putting our house on the market and had even begun the process of house hunting at the new location when suddenly, as God is wont to do, He reminded me of His wisdom, available to His child, just for the asking.

Reminded that I needed to seek His counsel and plan first, I stopped in my tracks and turned my focus to Him. As I prayed, He seemed to be overwhelmingly saying, "Wait."

My life verse should be, "If we are faithless, He remains faithful, for He cannot deny Himself" (2 Tim. 2:13 NASB). God is unchangeably faithful to who He is, what He tells us, and what He does. I am not this way. But He sticks with me anyway. That's humbling and amazing too.

So what does this learning to fast to seek God's guidance look like? For me, it looked like sitting quietly with my Bible and a cup of coffee. It often included having my journal open and praise music playing. It became fun to take a problem to Him, asking for His wisdom and expecting His help. I learned to listen to the ways He spoke to me through Scripture, where something I had read dozens of times suddenly jumped off the page and was filled with life. Or a song would play and I could sense the Spirit affirming the words to my spirit. Many times God's guidance came to me in the still of the night when I was seeking Him in intense prayer. I would ask Him to please speak and then often sense an overwhelming peace and the answer coming to me simultaneously. If you have never experienced any of this, don't worry. It takes time and practice to hear. Ask Him to help you, still yourself before Him, and listen. He is always there. His Spirit lives inside of you and is communicating His heart and His desires to you. I promise you, once you grow accustomed to hearing His voice, there is no other voice or perspective you would rather hear.

When I learned to fast, I learned to listen. I asked Him to *help* me listen. James 4:8 says, "Draw near to God and He will draw near to you. Cleanse your hands, you sinners; and purify your hearts, you double-minded" (NASB). When we fast, we have the opportunity to draw near to God, and He then draws near to us. We then can seek cleansing, because to be in His presence is to be aware of our sin. We next can have our hearts purified so that we won't be double-minded. And then, when we aren't double-minded and we ask for wisdom, He will generously give it to us. We can then go forward with no doubts! Isn't that great news?

Suzanne and I have talked about how we often hear God speak even outside of our prayer time. Sometimes we hear from Him while we are washing dishes or while driving or at the grocery store. Sometimes He comes to us in the middle of work to open our eyes to a truth He wants to share. We serve a generous God. He is always ready and willing to offer us help, guidance, and wisdom. We just need to ask Him and then wait for His answer, believing He will respond to us.

I have found that the role fasting plays is that it has given fervor to my prayers for wisdom. Fasting has helped me hear and act.

The amazing news is that the One who made you and knows how your mind works wants to be your rock. He is the all-wise God of the universe, and He wants to share His wisdom with you! Fast and pray for His wisdom, and the waves of doubt will be quieted by the One who rebuked and calmed a raging sea (Luke 8:24). Approach Him knowing that He is the one person in your life who actually wants to hear *everything* you have to say! Don't be afraid to go to Him with the menial and the major. If He can help me, a storm-tossed woman, He can most certainly help you.

The more you seek Him you will find this discipline becoming a highly addictive habit. The reason is that you see the results and they will amaze you. His wisdom in handling things is really far greater than ours. The more you see how applying His wisdom turns out, the more seeking it will become your default. You will want to pick up the phone and make a call less in your search for guidance. When needing to settle a sibling dispute or trying to comfort a hurting child or friend, you will find yourself shooting God a quick prayer, something along the lines of asking Him to put His words in your mouth (which is biblical! Read Isaiah 51:16). Then pause the few seconds it takes to listen. You will be amazed at the things you hear coming forth from your very own lips.

# Fast Food for Thought

- ↷ When you have a problem or concern, where do you usually turn for wisdom? How has that been working out for you?

- ↷ Will you commit to seeking God's counsel and learning to hear His voice so you can have His generous wisdom?

- ↷ Give God a try. Take that problem you are facing, that person you are struggling with, that situation at work … whatever it is, take it to God in prayer, seek His guidance in it, believe He will answer you, then listen for Him to speak.

- ↷ God gives you guidance; follow it. You never know how high He might ask you to climb, but you can be certain that He is directing your every step and using it for a good purpose.

*Dear Jesus, I confess my double-mindedness and the behaviors that result. I know I have sought wisdom in the world and from people who don't even know you or your Word. I have failed to come to you first, many, many times. Please forgive me for these behaviors. I want to repent and come to you for wisdom. As I fast, please focus my heart and tune my ear to hear your voice. Your wisdom is higher than any other, your voice is purer and sweeter than any other. Your ways are perfect. Please teach them to me. Help me walk in obedience once you have shown me your way. Help me also become a source of knowing your Word and sharing it with my friends and family when they come to me for help. I pray your words and your wisdom will rule my heart and mind this day. Please protect me from stepping out of your will and your wisdom. Let the enemy's voice sound like nonsense and let my flesh sound like foolishness to my mind. Thank you that you offer to give of your wisdom generously to me. In your name I pray, amen.*

## CHAPTER 6

# Fasting as an Act of Worship

*F*asting and worship go together like a hand in a supple leather glove, but we didn't know how good the fit was until we started fasting.

## From Wendy

On a day of fasting, I was struck with a desire to offer my empty food plate as a sacrifice of worship to the Lord. He had been so good to me the day before. It had been a day of rare attack and unqualified failure on my part. As always, He forgave my iniquity, and I wanted to show Him my love and gratitude. I was overwhelmed by His grace and just wanted to love Him with an act of prayer and worship. If Jesus had been with me then in his human state, I would have longed to pour the vial of perfumed oil on His feet as Mary did centuries before (John 12:1–3). Instead, I found myself asking Him if I could pour myself out at His feet and love Him with a freshly broken yet exceedingly grateful heart. He is so worthy, and I am so in need of more of Him and less of myself. He had lovingly cared for me through a day of pain and rebellion. I knew I had only come through it by His mercy and just wanted to offer a sweet aroma of sacrifice to rise before His throne. I felt as the Psalmist had: "Let them give thanks to the Lord for His lovingkindness, and for His wonders to the sons of men!" (Ps. 107:21 NASB).

Preceding my day of fasting was "The Day of Selfish Disaster." I had been disobedient in my attitude, emotions, and words due to a hurt I felt justified to harbor. I was deceived by my emotions and spent much of the day in complete focus on myself. Anger, hurt, and complaint became the standard for the day. Though I felt the Lord wooing me to prayer and His Word, I resisted Him and stepped further into disobedience and the quenching of the Spirit.

Let me just tell you, to quench the Spirit is a steep and slippery slope. Once we have turned a deaf ear to His pleading, His voice is harder and harder to hear through the lies of the enemy and the cacophony of our self-righteous flesh. Even when we know better, Satan's skill with well-aimed arrows, wielded to encourage focus on our wounded pride, can be tempting. On this day they became for me the siren call to abandon dying to myself and instead veer headfirst into the deadly waters of the sea of pride.

Some of the circumstances leading to my self-focus and rebellion were insidious, while still more were completely obvious ploys of the enemy. By the end of the day and some serious Bible time, prayer time, confession, and intercession by Suzanne and others, God had me just where He wanted me—broken and seeing my own righteousness as the filthy rag it was. I finally saw that I was far from justified in my feelings of injury and self-righteousness. Through my pain, I had allowed the enemy to convince me that I was right to say hurtful things to others because they "needed to be said." Oh, if I had only remembered that fasting meant to "cover one's mouth"! Through His Word, the Lord began to heal my heart and remind me of the white robe of His righteousness He had lovingly draped over my filth and nakedness.

How could I not love this God? How could I not want to fall at the feet and adore this Jesus? He never condemned me through the whole day, though He did discipline me and rebuke me with His truth. He waited for me to repent and come to Him with obedience and sadness over my sin so that He could welcome me home like the prodigal I had been all day long. I was truly saddened by my own failure and behavior. Yet, from my Lord, all I felt was love.

So how fun and how special it is to take a portion of a day to honor Him. Not to spend a day giving Him all of my requests, but to instead give Him all of my praise. To let praise music fill my home and car. To remember something new to thank Him for every time my stomach growled throughout the day. How great to choose joy, just so it would please Him, all day long, regardless of life's stressors. It is an awesome and refreshing way to spend a day!

*Fasting and prayer in this situation, and many others besides, have taught me to offer praise and worship for the sheer joy of being humbled by and thankful for God's presence.*

# From Suzanne

Many weeks into my fasting routine with Wendy, the Lord taught me that fasting is not a routine at all. He led me back to Isaiah 58 as a reminder that genuine fasting is what He says it is, not what I make it.

I am so thankful for Scripture and the examples we have in our spiritual heritage. I have found in my studies that God can sometimes tell you to do something that doesn't make sense. Like when He promised Abraham that he would be the father of many nations and then told him to sacrifice the only means he had of carrying on the family name. Or consider Joshua, a great battle strategist and mighty warrior who had led battles under Moses. Do you think he might have been a bit concerned over why God wanted him to fight a battle with marching, trumpets blaring, and shouts? Scripture gives us no indication that Abraham and Joshua responded to God with doubts over what He told them to do and expect. While I know I am in this family of believers, for me the family resemblance ends there. On one day when I heard God speak to me, I tried to excuse His voice away because what He said didn't make immediate sense.

It was on my fasting day with Wendy. We had spent precious time on the phone the previous night catching up and sharing prayer requests. Then we agreed that the following day we would not eat, but we would pray, study, and catch up with each other later in the day to see how our time went. I had also already planned to answer the request of a friend who wanted to get together and pray for an hour in the afternoon. Because my afternoon was full, I started my day early. I got up and had my quiet time with the Lord. I worshiped, prayed, and kept asking the Holy Spirit to give me strength to resist the temptation I felt while I fired up the Crock-Pot and loaded it up with food and spices that I wanted to eat but had already forsaken for the day. I also asked to hear God's voice. And I did, not audibly, but that still, small whisper. Here's how the conversation went.

*God:* "I want you to worship me."

*Suzanne:* "Great idea, Lord. You got it. When my friend gets here, I will share with her that you want us to worship, and then we can pray together."

*God:* "I want you to only worship today."

*Suzanne:* "But the Bible says we have not because we ask not."

*Okay, let's consider the audacity of me, the reader, quoting the Author's material back to Him for the sake of explaining His own words to Him.*

*God:* "I know what you need before you ask, and today I only want you to worship."

*Suzanne:* "Yes, Lord. Of course you're right. We will love to worship you."

*God:* "And I want you to prepare and take communion."

*Suzanne:* "Okay, I can do that. I have grape juice and bread … oh wait, I can't."

*God:* "What do you mean you can't?"

*Suzanne:* "I'm fasting, remember? So no communion."

*God:* "Who's in charge here? I'm not asking you to have a ten-course meal, but I am asking you to remember my body that was broken for you, my blood that atoned for your sins, by sharing in communion. And then I want you to pray and ask that I will make you broken bread and poured-out wine for my glory."

*Whoa! I heard that one loud and clear. And without having time to ask exactly what that might mean, I was drawn to obeying Him.*

*Suzanne:* "Yes, Lord, thank you Lord, of course Lord. But I better call Wendy and just let her know what you want me to do."

*What I was really doing was picking up the phone to get Wendy's permission. Since God knows our thoughts even before we do, He was ready with an answer.*

*God:* "NO, do not call her. You are accountable to me for this one, not Wendy. I will teach her, just as I am teaching you, and hers may be a different lesson today. That is up to me."

*Suzanne:* "But, but, uh …"

*God:* "You have something to add?"

*Suzanne:* "I'm assuming that after I have the communion, I can eat, my fast is over. Right?"

*God:* "No, my child. You fulfill your commitment with Wendy and me, and continue the fast until the time you both decided on. Communion is not to speak to your body; it is to speak to your soul."

*Suzanne:* "Oh, Jesus, thank you. I'm beginning to get it now. Please help me obey. Thank you for speaking to me, teaching me, correcting me, and loving me. I guess I better go get communion ready."

*God:* "I'll be looking forward to receiving you and accepting your sacrifice."

*Suzanne:* "Sacrifice? Are you talking about fasting, or asking something new of me? What kind of sacrifice?" (For some reason, at that point there was silence.)

The Lord is always with us and desires to speak to us and teach us. But we must seek Him and put Him first. We must rely on Him when we want more than anything to eat a Twinkie. What we give up is nothing compared to what we get in return. So the moral of the story is: Listen for God with open ears, be teachable, and above all, remember who's boss!

Well, I went upstairs to get ready for my friend to come when I received a call that her car wouldn't start, so she wouldn't be joining me for prayer that day. Does this mean that I had not heard from the Lord earlier? Should I doubt I'd had a conversation with Him? No, but it made me wonder if He had other plans for me, or if what had happened with my friend's car had been part of His plan all along. So, I spoke to Him again.

*Suzanne:* "Okay, Lord, did I misinterpret something? I really am sure you wanted me to worship and have communion with my friend."

*God:* "I said I wanted *you* to worship and have communion."

*Suzanne:* "By myself?"

*God:* "No, I'll be here too. Don't you remember reading that devotional that talked about being broken bread and poured-out wine, and how you said you wanted that? You wanted to make a sacrifice for me?"

*Suzanne:* "Yes, Lord, but I was scared to really offer it because of what it might mean."

*God:* "Would you like to find out what it means?"

*Suzanne:* "Yes, but can I find out what it means before I make the commitment?"

*God:* "You can't find out what it means until you make the sacrifice. Place yourself in my hands and I will show you."

This is where God led me to Scripture passages talking about the Passover and the Last Supper. Although I had read these accounts before, this time they had a new meaning for me. They helped me understand that I needed to make a personal decision about how far I was willing to go for Jesus. Can I believe God enough for me to make a commitment? Can I trust Him enough to lay myself on the altar and let Him take me wherever that leads? Deep in my heart, I knew that I could not really live any other way. I was beginning to get the message that on this day, my worship was about making a covenant with the Lord. It was to be something just between Him and me.

So, I went upstairs and prepared for communion. I felt led to set the atmosphere by lighting some candles, closing the blinds, and preparing a quiet place to meet with God and make some decisions. I got on my knees and admitted that I wasn't sure what I was doing. Graciously, Jesus led me through it and gave me the words. As I took the bread, I thanked Him for His broken body. Knowing all too well that it should have been mine, my gratitude led me to pray to be broken bread for His service. I then took the cup and thanked Him for his blood, asking Him to bathe me in it. I thanked Him for spilling it for my redemption so I could be forgiven and saved and come to know Him. Then I asked to be poured-out wine to bring glory to His name.

This was the Lord's timing and choice of worship. I was afraid to pray this way before that day, but Christ gave me a peace and a desire to lay my life down for Him. Don't get me wrong. Agreeing to be broken bread and poured-out wine, that was hard at first. But entrusting Him with my very life— that was the best decision I ever made!

*Fasting and prayer have taught me not to assume that just because I have set aside my day that I know how God wants me to conduct it. I need to listen for His voice because He just might have a directive for how He wants to be worshipped. He always knows best!*

# WORSHIP WAYS

We want you to know that one of our favorite ways to praise and worship God is to pump up the worship music and just dance before the Lord, praising Him in all circumstances, knowing that every chain has been broken. This is worship in the spirit of Psalm 149:3, "Let them praise His name with dancing; Let them sing praises to Him with timbrel and lyre" (NASB).

The Lord deserves our praise and worship, and it is pure joy to offer it to Him. What a privilege we have to be called daughters of the King!

We know that there will be some days you will feel like a princess, fully loved and fully blessed. And there will be other days you will feel fully worthless and fully a mess. Know this: whatever our feelings are, our position as His daughter has not changed. Our circumstances, sin, grumbling, or poor attitude cannot change that.

We have learned a wonderful blessing during fasting: you can take a reprieve of focusing on yourself and your condition for the day, and instead turn your attention to your position in Christ. In doing that, you may just find yourself with fresh wonder and love for Him. If so, praise Him!

There are going to be times when you do not feel like fasting. These are opportunities you have to sacrifice your day of fasting as a thank offering to Christ. Even if you begin your day with "sacrifice" as your foremost thought, and let's be honest, some days you will, to think of the day as a chance to thank Him and praise Him for his unfailing love and wonderful deeds will *change you*. Try it and see if by the end of the day you just aren't telling of His works with songs of joy.

# Fast Food for Thought

- ☙ Take some time to read through Isaiah 58. Note the kind of fasting God dislikes, and contrast that with the kind of fasting He says He desires. Ask Him to help you understand the passage and to see His heart for you in fasting.

- ☙ When was the last time you set aside an hour or even an entire day to devote to doing nothing else other than praising God and basking in His presence? Consider when you can do this, perhaps for an hour or two, a half day, or even a full day.

- ☙ What type of worship draws you to the heart of God? Have you ever tried asking Him to lead you into His choice of worship? Give Him the lead and see what He does with it.

*Dear Jesus, I sing for joy to the Lord, I shout aloud to the Rock of my Salvation, I come before you with thanksgiving and extol you with music and song. For great are you, Lord, the great King above all gods. Come let us bow down in worship, let us kneel before the Lord our God our Maker, for He is our God. In your name I pray, amen. (Adapted from Ps. 95)*

CHAPTER 7

# Fasting for Your Marriage

*W*e all dreamed about marriage, even as little girls and teens. We talked about what color our bridesmaids would wear, what our dress would look like, and how perfect our wedding would be. All we needed was the man who would sweep us off our feet. The arrival of the tall, handsome prince who would treat us like a princess for the rest of our life.

The world and Disney have concocted a vision of love and romance that really sets all of us females up for disappointment. Be honest, how many Princesses and Prince Charmings do you know personally? How many castles are there in your suburban tract? And even if this view of marriage were true, it still would never come close to having a Christ-centered marriage where two come together to love one another the way God intends them to. God created marriage to be a fulfilling love relationship where self-denial is an act of love. God's design is for a partnership where husband and wife put the other ahead of oneself and live in faithfulness and servanthood to each other. That is far better than the fantasy portrait so many of us dreamed about.

Of course, a real marriage comes with responsibilities, not just expectations. And for us Christians, some of these responsibilities are spiritual. Once we, Wendy and Suzanne, started fasting, the way we prayed for our husbands took on a new depth. It was the cry of our hearts that our husbands grow in the Lord, that they know their identity in Christ, that they love the Word of God and serve the Lord wholeheartedly. And we came to realize that if we, as their wives, did not pray fervent prayers for them, who would? If you want to see your husband live the life God created for him, to be truly transformed into the man God desires him to be, then you must consistently pray for him. You certainly cannot persuade, cry, trick, or nag him into the man you want and God intends him to be. That type of attitude and approach is outside of the character of Christ and *never* has a positive or life-altering effect. Trust us, we have both tried some of those methods, and they don't work. Look, there are no perfect marriages, but if you want a truly godly marriage, then you need to spend serious time on your knees. Satan wants nothing more than to destroy the family, and that starts with destroying the marriage.

Suzanne knew a couple serving overseas with a ministry organization. One morning, while the wife's husband was working in one ministry capacity, his wife decided to visit a nursing home to bless some elderly folk who lived there. As she entered, she saw a circle of older people sitting together and praying. She approached them to vocally applaud their commitment to rise so early in the morning to pray to Jesus.

An elderly woman turned to her and said, "We aren't praying to Jesus; we are praying to Satan for the destruction of Christian marriages in America."

We are in a war, fighting "against the spiritual forces of evil in the heavenly realms" (Eph. 6:12). And to fight it, we need spiritual weapons, such as prayer (v. 18). We need to be on our knees, praying for our marriages.

## From Suzanne

*Fasting and prayer have taught me that it is my responsibility as a wife to pray for, encourage, honor, and respect my husband. God has encouraged me to obey the guidelines He sets for wives in His Word, and He has proven to me that the reward is a Christ-centered marriage and children who grow up to be godly.*

The apostle Paul says, "Each individual among you also is to love his own wife even as himself, and the wife must see to it that she respects her husband" (Eph. 5:33 NASB). Aretha Franklin made the word R-E-S-P-E-C-T a household word. It's an important word. And Paul calls on those of us who are wives to respect our husbands. However, let me say before we venture any further on this subject, you are not required to respect a husband who abuses you or commits adultery. In those cases, I urge you to get help and counsel right away.

Ever since the garden of Eden and the Eve incident, we were destined to a couple of things recorded here: (1) a painful delivery in childbirth and (2) a "desire" for a husband who will "rule" over us (Gen. 3:16). Although this was part of the curse due to sin, knowing I serve a loving God, I prefer to look at the upside. I may experience pain in childbirth, but the result is a precious child, a gift from God. My husband is determined by God to be the head of the home, but in God's Word, I am to be his helpmate. That means we work together, discussing options and decisions, but ultimately he will have the final say. If he is a true Christ follower, then you can rest with peace in his choices. If not, then this is a good reason to pray for godliness in your husband. You will receive great benefit from the fruit of that prayer.

Loving a husband who loves you as God commands, as Christ loved the church (Eph. 5:25), can come easy for us. But what about respect? Not so much. God does command it, and it is our responsibility to obey that command. So naturally that means that we should do our best to try and change them, encourage them to be the man we think they should be, prod and push them until they reach their full potential even if it kills them … *whoa!* Now that is just so very wrong, but isn't this what most women do?

Let's consider a different approach—a way that will actually work and endear your husband to you. This approach is all about praying over your desires for your marriage and your need to respect your husband and allowing God to bring about the result. Instead of hounding your husband until the sound of your voice becomes likened to nails on a chalkboard, we suggest setting your goal toward becoming his prayer warrior. It works far better, girls, when God is the one whispering in your man's ear. I have seen God work in my husband through prayer that might not have come to pass if I would have just pushed my agenda. I have also seen how this type of spiritual discipline can reveal that God is speaking to both my husband and me about the same heart in ministry.

Several years ago, I had a deep desire to have a home that we could use for youth, a place in which they could hang out and learn of God's love. I secretly prayed about this and the amenities that would interest youth in spending time at the Niles abode.

The day came when my husband expressed and actually pursued making this happen. I can now think back to several years involving precious times of a youth group of thirty to fifty middle school kids staying at our home for a three-day camp and watching a group of ninety high school students emerge from our basement. Those years were not only life changing for us but for our children as well. They watched the joy we received by sharing what God had so graciously provided for us.

We truly believe it is your God-given responsibility as a wife to pray for your husband daily. And just in case you are harboring any ill feelings or offense toward your man, praying for him will truly not only change him but your attitude toward him. In fact, it is highly probable that God will work on and change more than your attitude—He will change you too.

Here are some suggestions for areas of prayer:

- Pray that God will bring your husband into the complete revelation of who God created him to be.
- Pray that your husband will seek God, always inquiring of Him and obeying.
- Pray for your husband to have wisdom and favor with God and man.

- Pray for his protection and that he will not fall into sin.
- Thank God for your husband. The more you do, the more you will realize all that you have to be thankful for. It is a game changer, and you will truly begin to be more and more grateful. That said, if you are being mistreated by your husband in any way, whether the abuse be physical or verbal, or if he is a "wanderer with the ladies," then please seek prayer support and counsel immediately. God instructs husbands in His Word how to treat their wives, and He grieves when there is harm done. A destructive marriage is *not* God's plan for you!
- Pray that God will love your husband through you. Ask Him to help you convey love, grace, and forgiveness beyond a human level.
- Ask God to fight your battles for you, show you where you need to change, and consistently commit your husband and your marriage to the Lord.

Especially in regards to that last one, there may be times in your marriage when the season is dark. The trials of life or one spouse's sin may cause an effect in the other spouse's life that is hurtful. Maybe the hurt is so deep that you can't even pray. In those times, if you have a Fast-Friend relationship, then your prayer partner can pray for you. There are even times when, because they are slightly removed from your immediate situation, they can pray the tough-love prayers that you can't bring yourself to pray.

Above all, love Jesus first and your husband second. If you do this, your desire to please Christ will motivate what you do and say and your relationship will benefit greatly. It is a misconception that any human person can complete us or make us happy. The expectations we put on one another to be exactly what that other person needs is unfair and impossible. Just imagine your daily life if you were consumed by trying to make your spouse into everything you needed. It would be a living nightmare and a completely unachievable goal. There is only one who can fulfill everything we need, and His name is Jesus.

Once we come to the reality and commitment that Jesus is our first love, I believe it frees us up to love our marriage partner in a more Christlike and edifying way—the way that allows a marriage to truly flourish. Seek Him. Love Him. Sacrifice for Him. In exchange you will receive more blessings than you could ever imagine.

## From Wendy

*Fasting and praying have taught me that my marriage has been one of the tools God has used to completely change me and draw me closer to Him. It is a precious truth to see that Jesus is enough, even during times when our marriages go through seasons of deep pain.*

I want to speak about praying and fasting during the times of your marriage when all is not well. When there is pain, heartache, confusion, or desperation. These are the moments you will find that your fasting and prayers sustain you and bring you peace and joy that no human help or human wisdom could ever equal.

No marriage is without seasons of loneliness or pain of some sort. Through my own experiences, as well as walking through dark times with several close friends, I know that there will be a time in every married woman's life when she needs the reminder of these beautiful words of God to His people: "For your husband is your Maker, whose name is the Lord of hosts. And your Redeemer is the Holy One of Israel, who is called the God of all the earth. For the Lord has called you, like a wife forsaken and grieved in spirit, even like a wife of one's youth when she is rejected" (Isa. 54:5–6 NASB). Pain pushes us to run or to become paralyzed. If in those moments you can train yourself to run to the Father or be paralyzed in stillness before Him, He will speak to you and reassure you. He will remind you that you are His daughter and He created you to carry yourself with the dignity of a child—a princess no less—of the most high God.

In your marriage, there may be times you know you are in a desert. You are having a fast, so to speak, imposed upon you. A fast from companionship with your spouse. A fast from intimacy. A fast from joy. A fast from trust or truth. I would encourage you to choose these moments to feast on the Word of God and on the peace of His presence as never before. You will reap a great reward in learning to see your God as your ultimate husband and Maker. He is *el roi,* the God who sees.

Now I want to raise the subject of divorce. If statistics are correct, then half of all women reading this book, even as Christians, will have had to suffer the pain and anguish of divorce or will in the future. No one goes into a marriage thinking it will end in divorce, so God, being our loving Father, knows how painful it is. It tears at our sense of self, our sense of worth, our security, our future. It rips apart what He has joined together, and regardless of how or why it happens, it hurts. Especially if your children are hurting too. There is no condemnation from Jesus, or from us, if you have been through divorce. The heart of the Father is so tender toward those who have had to go through the pain of it, whatever the cause.

In the case of a husband's ungodly treatment of his wife, Malachi 2 discusses God's view of divorce. In these verses, God says He hates it and that He sees and acts as a witness when a husband treats treacherously the wife of his youth. Ladies, God is your champion. If your husband has not honored his vows to you, God noticed. If you feel you were responsible for some or all of the reason your marriage fell apart, God has great compassion and grace for those who turn to Him and ask Him to redeem the situation for His glory and their good. This may not involve reconciliation for your marriage, but it could mean a healthy trust in God for what is ahead. If children are involved, the tender heart of their heavenly Father is filled with love and healing for them. Turn to Him and turn this matter over to Him. Who better than God to cover and repair the broken hearts we have and see in the ones we love? And what more could we want?

If you have suffered through a divorce, whether it was your choice or your husband's to end the marriage, there is still hope. One of my dear and beautiful friends in Christ prayed faithfully for her husband for eight years to be protected from repeated temptation and to be drawn to Christ. Her husband ended up leaving her for another woman anyway. This happens. She will tell you, however, that though her husband chose another path, God changed her through the process of praying and fasting for him. She drew so close to the heart of the Father that when the marriage finally ended, she stood equipped in His power and grace, ready to go forward on her own with God. Today she is a very happy woman in a new relationship. Her children love the Lord and are doing very well in college and careers.

While her story illustrates hope, it also shows that even when you are faithful, your spouse may leave. I want to reassure you that if your marriage does not turn out like your hopes and dreams, despite your faithful prayers, *you did not fail God*. The issue wasn't that you didn't fast, pray, hope, or believe hard enough. It's just that your husband has free will, just like you. Your husband failed *you*; it was his choice.

Also know that *God did not fail you!* God did not turn away from your broken voice crying out to Him through tears. He caught every tear. He heard every cry. He is gently and tenderly holding each piece of your broken heart. And He has a plan. It is for your good and His glory. Your joy is coming. Your dark night will end and morning will come. Hear these words from the Isaiah chapter on fasting and take them to heart: "Then your light will break out like the dawn, and your recovery will speedily spring forth; and your righteousness will go before you; the glory of the Lord will be your rear guard" (Isa. 58:8 NASB). What an awesome verse filled with powerful promises. God is the light. He is the One bringing healing and recovery.

He is the truth that goes before you. And my favorite, His very own glory will follow and defend you! Ladies, He has got your back. Rest easy and keep looking to Him.

I also want to speak on temptation in marriage. It is highly likely that each married person will come across a man or a woman with whom there is a temptation to stray. With the proliferation of social media, Web sites designed to make meet-ups easy for the single or the married, texting, Skyping, and so much more, finding someone to connect with outside of your marriage is easier than ever. If you ever feel as if you have crossed some lines and don't feel like making the trek back to safety (after all, temptation seems awfully fun and completely justified sometimes), then ask God to pull you back. He can, and He will rescue you—if you are willing. Fasting will help you tune your ear and radar to the still, small voice of the Spirit. Fast for the power to get out of, or be released from, temptation yourself. Do the same for your husband. Remember, God is mighty to save.

When agony or despair hit, don't panic—pray! When everything in you screams that you are being wronged, don't fight—fast! One of my favorite verses is Exodus 14:14: "The Lord will fight for you while you keep silent" (NASB). There it is again, that whole notion of *tsum*, fasting as covering my mouth. Many wives have told me, and reiterated the truth, that their voices are not often the ones that move their husbands to change or action. Rather, it is the voice of the One and Only. My sin gets in the way of my words too easily, especially with my husband when emotions are running high. The last thing I want is to have a new pile of things to confess because

I have lost control and spoken in self-righteous anger (the most seductive and tempting kind because it feels so right). Fasting became a way for me to learn to be quiet and let God fight. It helped me walk away and pray. Fasting would consistently show me where I was at fault in my marriage and when I needed to seek forgiveness for the injuries I had caused.

I have met six lovely, godly women this past year, all of whom are victims of infidelity. I have watched them draw close to the Lord as never before as a result of this time of searing pain. If we allow Him, God can use even the most devastating blow to rebuild our marriages and us into something that brings Him glory.

Fast and pray that He will guard your heart from bitterness, rage, hate, and debilitating despair. The enemy comes to steal, kill, and destroy. Fast from the emotions, thoughts, and beliefs you know come from the enemy and the world. Instead, feast on God's faithfulness and on His ability to cause streams to spring forth in the desert. Make this a conscious choice, because I guarantee it doesn't come naturally. These are the moments and hours that your faith muscle will be tested. Be glad for the strength you have gained through learning to habitually run to the Father and spend time with Him in prayer and fasting. He will grant wisdom and peace during the storm.

# FAST FOOD FOR THOUGHT

- ❧ Do you want a Christ-centered marriage that is blessed by God? Then you must pray consistently for and respect your husband. Be his biggest cheerleader and ask God to make him yours!

- ❧ If you are in a season of pain in your marriage, will you commit to seek the Lord through fasting and prayer and let Him minister healing and hope to you? Pray for your marriage or for someone else's to be protected from temptation today.

- ❧ If you are on the backside of a marriage that has ended in divorce, don't despair. Take time to pray and fast for God's insight, receive His healing grace, and seek His guidance for future relationships.

*Dear Jesus, I thank you for my husband and how you are working in his life. Please help him to move into the purpose you created him for and be a man after your own heart. Help me to know your Word as it pertains to me as a wife so that I honor you and respect my husband. Please help us keep you at the center of our married life. Please guard us from temptations. Help us be centered in you. When seasons of pain come, please help us to run to you. In your name I pray, amen.*

## CHAPTER 8

# Fasting for Your Children

Children are a blessing from the Lord. They are precious and precocious, full of life and yet sometimes drain ours. They are a great responsibility and also a great gift. Giving birth to them may be painful, but no matter how hard the delivery, once we see that sweet little baby, the memory of our pain subsides pretty quickly and is overrun with an overwhelming amount of love.

## From Suzanne

Since I am older than Wendy, my kids are older than hers. I have enjoyed giving her input that will hopefully help her avoid my mistakes and also prepare her for the different behaviors and attitudes that can go with different phases of a child's life.

Along with getting advice from others, both of us have prayed for our children from the moment we found out we were pregnant with them, and God has been incredibly good in answering those prayers and showing us evidence of His goodness. We have also sought to give our children wise, godly training. The Bible states in Proverbs 22:6 that if we "train up a child in the way he should go, even when he is old he will not depart from it" (NASB). Since my kids are now in their twenties, I can tell you that fasting and praying for them is one of the best uses of my time as a mom. Praying Scripture for them was also something that God proved faithful to answer. I chose to pray Luke 2:52 for each of them, asking that they would grow "in wisdom and stature, and in favor with God and man" as Jesus did.

After seven years of marriage, my husband and I realized that it was time we started our family. But having a child didn't come easily. I suffered a bout of endometriosis and ended up needing surgery. The doctor said it could be years before I would conceive, if ever, and then I would most likely miscarry. To say his bedside manner was lacking would be an understatement!

After a matter of months, we proved him wrong: I became pregnant. God blessed us with a beautiful little boy whom I did not immediately give back to Him. In 1 Samuel 1, Hannah made a promise to God that if she bore a son, she would give him back for God's service. Hannah followed through on that promise. I, on the other hand, was no Hannah. Oh, I told people I had given my son back to God. My husband and I even made a public confession of giving Tyler to God when we had him dedicated at our church. But my parents tended to be fearful in how they raised me and I followed suit. The days, months, and years of being overly protective and worrisome began. When my husband would try to correct my concern, I let him know in no uncertain terms that my behavior simply came with the territory and that all mothers were like this.

God knew I needed to see that He was and would remain in control whether I gave Him my children or not. I finally came to realize that given the choice of who could do a better job protecting Tyler, Travis, and Nicki, it was really a no-brainer choice. God won, hands down. After all, He could be there 24/7. What more could a mom ask for?

When I finally gave my children over to God, realizing that He would be there all the time for them, peace flooded my soul. My job as a mother came into perspective. I was given the position of loving them, training them, praying for them, and living my life sacrificially for Jesus in front of them. To do this, I needed the strength of the Lord, because I would totally mess it up on my own. So I looked to Him daily, asking Him to teach, speak to, and empower me in the training of my children. One of the most powerful truths I ever learned from a brilliant Christian speaker was "whatever you want your kids to be, *be that.*" In other words, your children may not always listen to you, but they will surely pick up your habits, good and bad. Prayer and fasting only strengthened my intercession for my children, and through those practices God empowered me to live a life daily before my children that would be an example of Christ. And when I would blow it, God humbled me to confess and ask for their forgiveness, which was a great lesson to them of repentance and God's faithfulness to redeem us.

God blessed me with a godly, even-tempered, and super-easy-to-get-along-with husband. Bob has been faithful to God in his demonstration of a life lived for Jesus in front of his children. I will always remember a time on vacation when the kids were nine, thirteen, and sixteen. Bob asked us all to sit on a couch in the hotel room. He then left the room and returned with a towel and a basin of water. He proceeded to wash each of our feet, just as Jesus had done for the disciples (John 13:5–20). You could have heard a pin drop in that hotel room. Each of us had tears in our eyes, sharing in this experience of being shown such great love. The fact that this man, husband, and father served us all in this way made an impact that will stick with all of us forever.

Just as you and I have done, our sons and daughters will reflect on their own fathers and their relationships with them as they develop their relationship with the heavenly Father. If you had an ungodly father, don't be discouraged. Our heavenly Father is bigger than the example you had, and I believe He will pour out His love, attention, protection, counsel, and more if you will let Him be that Father you never had. There is no limit to what God can do, regardless of your past or present.

While raising my children, God was refining me through fasting and prayer, and His Word became more alive to me than ever before. His grace in this allowed me to be in the right frame of mind to let His Holy Spirit lead me when there was a natural opening to grab a teachable moment with my kids. One day while driving Nicki to elementary school, I silently asked God to give me a word for her that would bless her that day. I very clearly heard, "Tell her how much I love her." So I did. Nicki got a smile on her face; it was a perfect mixture of peace, contentment, and fulfillment. Then Nicki started a conversation with me.

"Mom, Lauren has been really rude and mean lately," Nicki said. "I'm not playing with her because she is being rude to everyone!"

I reflected to myself how vile the tongue can be. As James 3:6 says, "The tongue also is a fire, a world of evil among the parts of the body. It corrupts the whole body, sets the whole course of one's life on fire, and is itself set on fire by hell." Maybe this girl meant to be cruel, but I always took the "everyone" comment with a grain of salt. I probed a bit, asking Nicki for some examples. I got a few, but not enough to determine why this friend Nicki had known since kindergarten was exhibiting this type of behavior.

I wanted to encourage Nicki's growth by working on character traits such as forgiveness, love, compassion, and grace, so I suggested that she love this person and pray for her. "Nicki, do you love God?" I asked.

"Of course I do, Mom."

"Well, the Bible says that if we love God, we should also love our brothers and sisters in Christ [1 John 4:19–21]. Jesus even tells us to love our enemies and to pray for those who hurt us [Matt. 5:44]. Now this girl is your sister in Christ. Maybe her walk with the Lord is a little off right now. Don't you think if Jesus wants you to pray for your enemies that it would make perfect sense to pray for your friends?"

Nicki voiced her agreement with this, but I felt the conversation should go one step further. "Nicki," I said, "please don't talk about her with the other girls."

"I won't, Mom," she said.

I then added: "If you want to talk to someone about this,

go to the person it concerns. I know that when you have been hurt sometimes, you don't want to see or talk to that person. You know, there were times when someone would hurt me, and I would think about hurting them back, but then I would remember how God feels about that. Romans 12:17 tells us to 'never pay back evil for evil to anyone. Respect what is right in the sight of all men' [NASB]. I know that both of us want to please Jesus and not cause Him to disapprove of our behavior. After all that Jesus has forgiven us, we must forgive also. You know when we pray the Lord's Prayer and we say the part about 'and forgive our sins as we forgive those who sin against us'? Think about that for a bit. Would you really want God to forgive you the way you forgive others? I know I wouldn't. I want God to forgive me in the way that only He can, and I want Him, in His power, to help me forgive the way that only He can.

"Once you have forgiven, ask for God to bless the other person. And ask God for a way you can minister to them. God commands in Luke 6:28 for us to bless those who curse us, to do good to those who hate us. Nicki, I know that God wanted you to understand how very much He loves you so that you could pass that love on to others today and bless them. Especially this friend who is hurting so badly that she allows her hurt to be a reason to hurt others."

I am so thankful to God that He prepared my heart and mind through prayer and fasting to bless and instruct my daughter this way. Nothing hits home like the truth of God's Word.

*Fasting and prayer have brought me comfort, joy, and peace over the years as I have prayed for my children and seen the mighty work of God in their lives and so many answers to prayer. Fasting and prayer have also taught me that God's Word is vital for life. When I take time to focus on God in a sacrificial way, my mind is more attuned to His truth and how I can share it with my children.*

## From Wendy

*Fasting and prayer have taught me that my kids have been the greatest source of joy and greatest level of responsibility I have felt. Fasting and praying for them has also focused my parenting. It has taught me to have a tender heart for weaknesses and a ferocious desire to see my children rooted and grounded in God's truth and love.*

Since Suzanne's kids are ten years older than mine, she has been a real mentor and source of wisdom and help in many areas. I love that she has been both my fast friend and my Titus-woman friend. We need more women like this in our lives. I adore her kids and can attest to the fact that they all are shining examples of Christ in the world.

I have probably logged more hours in fasting and praying for my kids than anything else. As women, we are blessed with an instinctive desire to protect our kids from everything. I can completely relate to Suzanne's issues with fear and overprotectiveness. But we cannot keep our kids from all hurts and dangers, no matter how hard we try. We need the Lord's help.

One of the most important aids God gives us is His Word.

Over the years, Suzanne and I have shared many Bible verses and used them during our prayer times and days of fasting, not just for us, but for our families. I have also spent countless times sitting with my Bible and a cup of coffee on a day of fasting, even for twenty minutes stolen before everyone wakes up, and asking God to lead me to certain verses to pray for my kids that day. My own mother's Bible has names next to many verses that she has claimed for her loved ones through the years. God's Spirit is alive, active, and moving. He knows—far better than we ever could—what our kids are going to face each day, what temptations they will have, what hurts they will encounter, and what opportunities they may be given.

How fun and awesome to ask God to guide you in how to fast and pray specifically for each child. Ask Him to tune your ear and your heart to get on the same frequency that your kids will hear. This is a huge request of mine. I often feel like Charlie Brown's teacher, making sounds no ear can decipher, when speaking to my children, Sydney and Robby. But when I can't break through, God can. In fact, I have learned how to be quiet more so I don't get in the way of the Lord speaking to my kids. Or even speaking to me!

Recently, I was listening to a sermon in which the pastor made a fleeting reference to the parable of the lost sheep in Luke 15. The parable states that the shepherd will leave the ninety-nine sheep in the safety of the pasture while he goes out and searches for the one lost sheep from his flock. While hearing this, I suddenly had a vision of myself telling the shepherd that when it came to my kids or family, he could take the night off and I would go out and find them. I would be responsible for their search and rescue. There I would be, tromping across rocks and untold dangers, until I finally found Sydney or Robby (or my husband, or whomever!) and stood there, hands on hips, berating them for being outside of the pasture, telling them all the reasons they should have known better than to leave their safe surroundings. Telling them, in no uncertain terms, *to get back in that pasture, NOW!* And then watching in bewilderment as they actually ran farther away from me!

God used this vision to remind me that I am to stay in the safety of the pasture, too, and to pray for His voice to be the one my family hears. I love the promise in John 10 where Jesus assures us that His sheep hear His voice and they will not go with another. As moms, certainly there are times we must teach, instruct, guide, admonish, and correct our children. That's part of the job description.

However, when one of my kids has an attitude of rebellion or stubbornness—if it seems as if their hearts are hardened in that moment—I know now that it is God's will to conduct the search and rescue. It is His voice they will hear. He is the gentle and good shepherd. I am the angry and often punitive mother! No wonder my children were running farther away from me in my vision. Who could blame them?

When we are fasting and praying for God to speak to our kids and for His spirit to attune their ears to His voice, we are creating an opportunity for an eternal relationship to grow and grow. I, for one, want my children to learn to hear the heavenly Father's voice, even over mine. When they stray, as all kids will in one way or another, I want them to know that He is the gentle and loving shepherd and that He is calling them back. Not in condemnation, but in love and to safety. This is a huge relief to me. After all, I know I am sometimes inconsistent. I say things at times that I shouldn't. I can act like a completely flesh-controlled woman.

I don't want my children, though, associating God's beautiful words with my sometimes screeching tone. Let your fasting and praying guide you as to what to say to your children and when to say it. And if you realize that your words could do more harm than good—in fact, especially at those times—then go back to the prayer pasture and let God do the talking.

There are several things I love to fast and pray for my kids:

They will be given a great gift of faith. (1 Cor. 12:9)

They will love God's Word and study it. (Psalm 119)

They will be lifelong seekers of God and will search for Him with all their hearts. (Jer. 29:13)

They will hear God's voice and follow it, and also discern the voice of the enemy and flee from him. (John 10:4–5)

They will be authentic. They will live real lives with real testimonies in front of their peers. They will never be ashamed of the gospel. (Rom. 1:6)

They will be equipped properly to fulfill the good works God has created for them since before the foundation of the world. (Eph. 2:10)

They will live lives in awe of Him. They will want to

aspire to honor, show gratitude, and serve Him, for our God is a consuming fire. (Heb. 12:28–29)

They will not judge others. They will concentrate on the log in their own eyes before trying to help others with a splinter. (Matt. 7:1–5)

They will learn to put on the full armor of God and properly defend against the enemy or attack him as needed. (Eph. 6:10–18)

They will be rooted and grounded in love, so that they may be able to comprehend the breadth, length, height, and depth in knowing Christ's love and be filled up to all the fullness of God. (Eph. 3:16–19)

I encourage you to have a quiet time with the Lord and ask Him to focus and align your goals for your kids with His. This is hard to do in today's world, where we feel pressured that their preschool choices will impact their college acceptance! I have to constantly catch myself and pull out of this wrong thinking. If I can teach my kids to walk by faith and not by sight and to do the best with the gifts God has given them, then why should I worry at all about their futures? They will be following His leading, and what more could any parent wish for than that?

# Fast Food for Thought

🜪 Do you model the behavior that you want your children to exhibit? The closer you walk to Jesus, the closer they will also likely walk.

🕭 Do you spend concentrated time in prayer for your children? Ask the Lord to lead and guide you into ways He wants you to specifically pray for their growth in Him. Begin to pray that they will be drawn into a lifelong relationship of seeking Him.

🕭 Do you know the Word well enough to instruct your children in it at the moment they need it? Think about what you can do to become a better student of God's Word.

*Dear Jesus, thank you for my children. I am so blessed to be a mother. I am humbled to be entrusted with loving them and helping point them to you. Please give me your wisdom and grace as I approach this job. Draw my children to your heart. Protect them from the enemy, and use your Spirit to lead and guide them. Help them love your Word too! Thank you for your Word that gives us everything we need to follow you and live a life that reflects Christ. Help me become consistent in studying the Word and committing it to memory so I am ready to train and instruct my children in the way they should go. In your name I pray, amen.*

## CHAPTER 9

# Fasting to Break Bondage

We have mentioned our spiritual enemy many times so far. His name is Satan, also known as the devil. He is a deceiver and a destroyer, and we need to take him seriously. The apostle Peter warned believers about Satan long ago: "Be alert and of sober mind. Your enemy the devil prowls around like a roaring lion looking for someone to devour. Resist him, standing firm in the faith, because you know that the family of believers throughout the world is undergoing the same kind of sufferings" (1 Peter 5:8–9). The evil one has no mercy.

At the same time, we Christians can take comfort in the fact that the Lord is far greater than the devil, and He has already defeated our enemy at the cross. Satan has been fatally wounded; his destruction is assured. But until he is put away for good, his goal is to create misery and deception in your life and in the lives of those you love the most. Jesus said, "The thief comes only to steal and kill and destroy" (John 10:10). So we need to be on our guard.

When Jesus' disciples encountered a demon-possessed man and found that they could not exorcise the demon, Jesus explained to them that this particular demon could not come out without prayer and fasting (Matt. 17:14–21). Some battles require heavier ammunition than others! We have found that fasting adds tremendous fervor to prayer in our own personal battles. We don't know how or why this works. We just know it does. Sometimes a loved one or we may be held in some kind of yoke or bond of oppression. When we recognize that and then add fasting to our prayers, things happen. Powerful things.

Though our enemy is out to hurt us, we want to caution you not to give the enemy too much credit. I (Suzanne) have had a history of expecting spiritual attack when entering into certain ministry situations. A wise woman told me recently that just because I am doing ministry doesn't mean the enemy is going to bring a full-fledged attack against me. If that were true, and the attack was always vicious, many people would faint from ministry. Satan seeks to be destructive, but God is much more powerful.

Rather than fearing our enemy, we should strive to depend on God more and believe that He will bring about good, that He will give life. Romans 8:28 says, "And we know that God causes all things to work together for good to those who love God, to those who are called according to *His* purpose" (NASB). We believe that if we stay in an attitude of worship and thanksgiving during difficult times, we can cut off some of the enemy's methods at the onset. We actually count a thankful heart and a spirit of praise as part of our battle plan.

# From Wendy

*Fasting and prayer have taught me to value self-control as a tool for being able to withstand attacks and have the clarity and strength to fight back.*

For me, there is another key hidden in the above verses from 1 Peter that will really help avoid opening the door to the enemy. Interesting that Peter put to be "self-controlled" even before he put to be alert. It is easier for me to be alert than self-controlled. It really was an eye-opener to see that my self-control can and should come before alertness. But how wise and true! When I am lacking self-control, I am wide open to the enemy attacking me and in turn using me. When my mouth is open and I am lacking self-control, sin is going to happen. I will say something in anger or hurt that the enemy will use. If I do not have control over my mind and submit my thoughts to Christ, I will mull and stew and imagine and create thoughts that will war against Christ.

The enemy loves to see us scheme and stew. If I am lacking self-control and my guard is down, I am very susceptible to following my flesh and rationalizing my actions. I am also less tuned in to areas where my kids may need guidance or help. It becomes easier to let things slide than to be vigilant. Through fasting, and those small and sometimes big ways I deny myself, I have actually matured greatly in this area of self-control. Denying ourselves and being self-controlled make us stronger. When the enemy does start to prowl around, we begin to sense it. If, during fasting, we practice "covering our mouths," he has one less area he can attack. If we focus on Scripture, worship, and prayer, the enemy's effect on our lives for that period of time is paralyzed.

One inroad the enemy likes to use is our own sins. He likes to use our bad choices against us. He can heighten our guilt and shame, making us feel low and worthless. But we have a remedy. James tells us, "Confess your sins to one another, and pray for one another so that you may be healed. The effective prayer of a righteous man can accomplish much" (James 5:16 NASB). Suzanne is this safe place for me. I can confess my sins and struggles with her and receive back no condemnation, just understanding, compassion, and prayer support. I know she will pray for me. I know that when we have prayed together for battles we have faced, God has heard our prayers. And when we have added fasting to the mix, we have become women the enemy would rather avoid than mess with. We want our lives to reflect what a popular poster says: "Be the type of Christian that when your feet hit the floor in the morning, Satan says, 'Oh snap, she's up!'" You can be that kind of Christian too.

Don't underestimate the power that God has given us in Jesus Christ. As Paul tells us, "I pray that the eyes of your heart may be enlightened in order that you may know the hope to which he has called you, the riches of his glorious inheritance in his holy people and his incomparably great power for us who believe. That power is the same as the mighty strength he exerted when he raised Christ from the dead and seated him at his right hand in the heavenly realms" (Eph. 1:18–20). The same power that raised Jesus from the grave and seated Him at the Father's right hand of authority is the same power you and I have. Our enemy cannot come close to matching that! Draw on that power, and no earthly bondage will be able to hold back your testimony, your ministry, and your love for Him.

# From Suzanne

*Fasting and prayer have taught me to truly live with Christ as my absolute fulfillment, my true identity. To find security in this life and the next, I have only to look to Jesus.*

Because my upbringing was somewhat freewheeling, I always felt invisible in a way. I also chose to hide the fact that I felt out of control. I didn't always make the right choices. I kept looking for that thing that would bring me some satisfaction, some boundaries, some much-needed security. Overprotective boyfriends and controlling agents in the entertainment business provided me with what I thought I needed. I was searching for that something that would bring order into my life. Even when I was married to my sweet, supportive husband, I still occasionally had that out-of-control feeling. I didn't understand at the time that it was my relationship with the Lord that needed to provide the security I longed for.

Fortunately, God loved me enough not to leave me as I was. He allowed something in my life to train and encourage me. The problem was, I distorted what He was trying to fulfill in my spirit by allowing it to become an obsession. He brought martial arts into my life to teach me some things I desperately needed before I could be used in certain areas for Him, but the more I got involved, the more preoccupied I became with it. I found myself thinking about the sport most of the time. It gave me some of the things I had been searching for. I found acceptance because I was good at it, had gratification in the form of winning competitions, and received a working knowledge of respect and discipline. But I was slowly trading my identity in Christ to identify with the distorted belief I had become a martial artist. This didn't happen because Tae kwon do was at fault, much less anyone else associated with the sport. Even though this discipline had a good deal of positive influence on my children and me, I turned it into a little god in my life. Consequently, I became so miserable with it consuming me that I got on my knees and begged God to take it from me. I implored Him to rescue me with a way out.

So He delivered me through a wonderful ministry that won my heart. I was asked to handle local communications and media for a large faith-based event. I felt that God had really made a statement, taking the mess I had made lately of my Christian walk and allowing me to be His servant with this ministry. I immediately felt the desire to get myself right with the Lord. My time was now consumed with ministry meetings to plan and publicize the event. I believed I had finally found my calling, my niche, even my family in the team that had come to Spokane. But this new ministry became my new obsession. My focus on God took a backseat. This happened so subtly that I didn't even see it.

When the event finally took place, I was thrilled to see the crowds coming and the lives changed. The ten months I had spent preparing with this team had been some of the best of my life.

But when the event came to an end, I didn't anticipate the change that would come when they all left for the next city. All of a sudden, the ministry that I woke up excited about every morning was gone. I hit bottom, feeling I had been left behind. But the One I had neglected was still with me. God convicted me and has completely healed me of any need for anything but Jesus to be my identity, my everything. He has given me the ability to guard my heart as Proverbs 4:23 describes: "Watch over your heart with all diligence, for from it flow the springs of life" (NASB).

You will never have the relationship with God that He intends for you to if there is something taking His place in your heart. If something other than God is the center of your life, you need to remove it from that place. Be like Josiah, one of the kings of ancient Israel, who "removed all the abominations from all the lands belonging to the sons of Israel, and made all who were present in Israel to serve the Lord their God. Throughout his lifetime they did not turn from following the Lord God of their fathers" (2 Chron. 34:33 NASB). Serve Jesus with all you are and have. Be determined to sincerely make Him your first love, your eternal security, and your complete identity.

## Fast Food for Thought

⚴ Are you currently in God's Word to strengthen your faith? Use your times of fasting and prayer to comb His Word for promises and truths you can use to combat the enemy in times of attack.

🌀 Would you say that Jesus is first in your life? If so, is His place secure, or do you move Him to second or third place when different opportunities come your way? We have heard it said that ministry can become a winsome mistress. And so can a husband, children, work, play, or any number of other good things that can become an obsession. Inventory your life. Is Jesus really at the center? If not, why?

🌀 God can help you reorder your life to Him. Determine what takes first place in your life. Is it God? Fast before Him. He will give you what you need to follow Him fully.

*Dear Jesus, thank you for being my strong tower and shield. I don't know what I would do without you. Please help me to be strong to believe in the might of your power and your Spirit. Remind me when I am battling in my own strength and lend me yours instead. You deserve first place in my heart and life, because you know that is the only way I will be safe from myself and my enemy. Please draw me to your side and warn me when I am straying. In your name I pray, amen.*

## CHAPTER 10

# Fasting to Strengthen Your Faith

Whether the exercise is cardio, weights, dance, or even an organized recreational sport, our culture is so hyper health and appearance driven that working out has become a part of most people's daily lives. Now, working out our bodies can be a good thing, but even many Christians often spend more time working their muscles than strengthening their faith. We need stronger faith muscles. We need them because God doesn't want us to be content with mediocrity in our relationship with Him. Moving forward in the faith requires more developed faith muscles. Another reason we need more spiritual strength is because, even though life is often marvelous, at times it can be incredibly, shockingly bumpy. And often the bumps are times when our Refiner turns up the heat to burn up the dross in our lives and mellow the gold. You, precious one in Christ, are the gold He is seeking to refine. Will you let Him refine you? Will you trust Him?

You have probably already had days when you wanted to stay in bed with your head buried in a pillow rather than face another day. Maybe you were paralyzed by pain from circumstances out of your control. Maybe you experienced heartbreak, or a sudden change in your life, or an emotional pit that left you with sobs only the Holy Spirit could hear or interpret. We have been there too. We have lived through times and things we thought would kill us. We have felt the hand of God stretch us beyond what we thought we could bear, only so we would rest more securely in those safe and beautiful nail-pierced hands of Jesus.

## From Suzanne

*Fasting and prayer have taught me that the more I deepen my relationship with the Lord and see His answers to my prayers, the more my faith, confidence, and hope grow by leaps and bounds. These spiritual disciplines have also taught me that fear is no match for God. Whatever fire He uses to refine me, I know I can walk through it and come out the other side better for having gone through the flames.*

There are two instances of fire in the Bible that stand out to me the most. One occasion is when God appears to Moses in the burning bush (Ex. 3). Here the fire does not consume the bush, and it makes a huge impression on Moses. The other time is when Daniel's three friends—Shadrach, Meshach, and Abednego—are tossed into the flames for refusing to worship an idol, and the flames do not touch them at all (Dan. 3). In both situations, God's power is demonstrated. When the blaze begins, God shows up big time!

Before I started fasting and praying, my faith during the

fire was very weak. I would worry, I would ruminate, and I rarely praised Him through the heat. For example, when Nicki was born, she had two holes in her heart. Instead of immediately entrusting her to God, I wondered, *why my child?* My wise husband said, "Why not?" You see, he was already on board with trusting God for her life. But I treated her like a porcelain doll for many months until God gently convinced me that she was His and in His watchful care.

One of the greatest blessings during times of combustion was that Bob has fasted and prayed one day a week. His faith has given me much confidence and peace knowing that when times are hard, my husband was pressing into God. The Psalmist encourages us, "Let all who take refuge in you be glad; let them ever sing for joy. Spread your protection over them, that those who love your name may rejoice in you" (Ps. 5:11).

Speaking from where I am now, I can tell you that God has grown me through the fire by leaps and bounds. Tests and trials do not affect me like they did in the past. Intimacy with God has brought me security in knowing how much He loves me and that there is nothing He can't handle.

Just a few weeks ago, I was battling a possible cancer diagnosis. I went through several tests and retests, including a biopsy. I can honestly say that there was not a shred of fear because through the years of prayer and fasting I have come to truly know who my God is. He is loving and powerful, and He has a definite plan for my life that nothing will stop short. I knew in my heart that whatever the diagnosis, negative or positive, He would carry me through. It was so amazing to compare my reaction now to what it used to be and see the transformation that my God has brought about in me. I can thankfully say that what appeared to be cancer was a false alarm. I can also say that by this occasion, God had truly brought me to the point of not only fasting through the fire but praising Him through it. "Because of the Lord's great love we are not consumed, for his compassions never fail. They are new every morning; great is your faithfulness" (Lam. 3:22–23).

I honestly can't even begin to imagine my life without the love of my great Creator and His guidance. Every time I look back at seasons of struggle in my life, I see the same thing—God's presence, power, and faithfulness. He has always provided. I understand what the Psalmist wrote so long ago, and I can gladly say the words with him to my God: "You are my strength, I sing praise to you; you, God, are my fortress, my God on whom I can rely" (Ps. 59:17).

*God* has *always* been the Giver of hope in my life and that of our family. So Paul says, "Now may the God of hope fill you with all joy and peace in believing, so that you will abound in hope by the power of the Holy Spirit" (Rom. 15:13 NASB).

*God* has *always* equipped me for everything He has asked me to do: "Now the God of peace, who brought up from the dead the great Shepherd of the sheep through the blood of the eternal covenant, even Jesus our Lord, equip you in every good thing to do His will, working in us that which is pleasing in His sight, through Jesus Christ, to whom be the glory forever and ever. Amen" (Heb. 13:20–22 NASB).

*God* has *always* been the Author of my life and my Sustainer. As Paul declared to a crowd of skeptics, "He made from one man every nation of mankind to live on all the face of the earth, having determined their appointed times and the boundaries of their habitation" (Acts 17:26 NASB).

*God* has *always* been wise in His direction, for "Great is our Lord and abundant in strength; His understanding is infinite" (Ps. 147:5 NASB).

*God* has *always* loved me. As the Lord told the prophet Jeremiah, "I have loved you with an everlasting love; therefore I have drawn you with lovingkindness" (Jer. 31:3 NASB).

*God* has been and will *always* be faithful! "Know therefore that the Lord your God, He is God, the faithful God, who keeps His covenant and His lovingkindness to a thousandth generation with those who love Him and keep His commandments" (Deut. 7:9 NASB).

We serve an amazing God! With Him behind us, in front of us, beside us, and over and under us, we have all we need to develop faith muscles of steel.

What can you do to strengthen your faith so that when times of trial come you are ready to do battle? Fast and pray. Live in a state of thankfulness and worship. Study and memorize the Word. Then His Word will be right there in your heart, ready to minister to you as it strengthens your faith and speaks life into your soul. Like any other discipline, committing God's Word to memory will take some effort on your part. So get yourself some three-by-five cards or a notebook and start writing down the verses you would like to memorize. Carry them with you. Recite them throughout the day. Meditate on them. In time, God's Word will become a part of you. Your faith will increase. Your trust in the Lord will grow. You'll have faith muscles, baby!

# From Wendy

*Fasting and prayer have taught me that fires will come but God is there to use them to refine me and purify me. His Word will guide me and His Spirit will renew me. If I submit to the process, it will be a beautiful thing!*

Are Jesus—*the Word*—and the Bible—*His words*—the foundation you are building your faith upon? Suzanne and I have literally chosen to stand again and again on these two cornerstones of faith when everything else around us has seemed to crumble. We have chosen to set aside a day a week to wrap ourselves in His Word and to listen to His truth and words of comfort. We have chosen to fast and keep covenant with Him and one another, even on days we would rather crumble to our feet, not in worship, but in self-pity over the turns our lives have taken. The fasting and the sacrifice have become even more precious when it has been done in obedience and as a love offering. When we have experienced fasting through difficult days and trials, it has become the opportunity to say, "Jesus, I don't know what you are doing right now, but I trust that you are here and that you are working in ways I cannot see or comprehend. I trust you. I love you so very much."

Suzanne's experiences of fasting through the fire have truly been an inspiration to me. They have impressed on me steadfastness in Christ and the firm foundation of Jesus and His Word. She has learned sweet lessons from trusting through very trying circumstances.

I have had the blessing of learning sweet lessons from still another kind of testing. I want to share with you the freedom from a particular kind of trial that I repeatedly experienced and one that kept me in bondage until I began to fast and pray, living His victory. I'm talking about the area of fear.

Jesus told His disciples, "Peace I leave with you; My peace I give to you; not as the world gives do I give to you. Do not let your heart be troubled, nor let it be fearful" (John 14:27 NASB). Don't fear. Don't be troubled. For many years, this was easier said than done. When the fires come in a marriage, a job loss, a diagnosis, or any number of other situations in life, fear rushes in. Fear steals our peace and prevents us from trusting God. But through fasting and prayer, I have learned to seek God's Word for truths that have given me courage in the face of fear. Here are some of these:

> The enemy is going to try to kill me, steal from me, and destroy me. (John 10:10)
>
> Jesus has given me weapons to fight the enemy. (Eph. 6:10–17)
>
> We will encounter trials and troubles in this life. (James 1:2–4)
>
> Jesus is our firm foundation and cornerstone. (Eph. 2:20)
>
> God's grace is sufficient for all trials and tests. (2 Cor. 12:9)
>
> God wants to refine me. (Ps. 66:10)
>
> Jesus will never leave me or forsake me. (Heb. 13:5)
>
> Hope is available to me, and it is an anchor for my soul. (Heb. 6:19)

I am upheld by God's righteous, omnipotent hand. (Isa. 41:10)

I can trust Him completely. (Prov. 30:5)

I have loved Jesus for nearly forty years of my life. I knew He wanted me to trust Him and not fear. But I lived in terrible, testimony-destroying fear on many different occasions of my life. The ways the enemy and my own flesh would lead me into fear over trials was crippling. It destroyed my joy. It stole time away from my Lord and my family because I was simply too fearful and miserable to do much more than exist.

This pattern of fear took many shapes. Here are just a few examples. After Sydney's diagnosis with cerebral palsy, I lived in fear that something would happen to our son, Robby, after he was born. At eight weeks, I was preparing for his checkup and glanced through the baby book to see what milestones he should be achieving. I became gripped with the most horrible fear that he was blind. Sure enough, he could not track any object my family or I would put in front of him. I'll never forget torturing the poor child for two days with a penlight in a dark room just to see if he would follow the light (as suggested in the baby book, of course). Our enemy is ruthless. He even convinced me that I caused Robby's blindness because I had forgotten on a couple of occasions to put drops in his eyes. Our pediatrician is a sweet sister in Christ, and she was able to reassure me that I had not caused Robby to go blind and that I needed to stop worrying and give him time. That very night, he tracked an object. God is merciful and wonderful to His doubting children!

That episode of "blindness fear" was just the beginning of a long summer of fear. I went on to make another doctor test my daughter for leukemia because she had a fever and bruising. That same month I became convinced I had melanoma. I called in absolute panic to my dear friend in Christ, Betsy, our town's most in-demand dermatologist. She graciously squeezed me into her busy appointment schedule the next day, just so she could tell me I had two freckles. I worried for months once that I contracted HIV from a cuticle trim during a pedicure. Good grief. My family came to dread the times I would come to them in absolute panic over new fear that had gripped me.

Right before Sydney was to face her first treatment with Botox for her cerebral palsy, I was terrified. The Lord laid on my heart a desire to covenant with Suzanne to fast and pray. I was facing a real need and wanted a real partner in prayer and seeking the Lord. Little did I know how precious and freeing it would become to seek the Lord in this manner.

The words of the Lord in Isaiah 58 became especially meaningful to me concerning the freedom I began to experience from fear and doubting when trials or irrational fear started to cloud my thinking: "Is this not the fast which I choose, to loosen the bonds of wickedness, to undo the bands of the yoke, and to let the oppressed go free and break every yoke?" (Isa. 58:6 NASB). Yes, the fast God chose for me was to free my mind and my heart from the bonds of wrong thinking and the yoke of fear that had silenced my voice and quenched His Spirit. What precious freedom I began to find in Him! This happened as a by-product of seeking Him through prayer and fasting, especially praying to hear His voice in a new, fresh way. The more we fasted and prayed on a weekly basis and the more I hungered to seek Him in between, the more freedom I began to experience from fear. I will praise His name forever for proving Himself so powerful and personal in this way. When fear is removed from the times of walking through the fire, we are able to completely trust and rest in Him.

Our enemy is not creative. He was never given the power to create anything. Therefore, if he has successfully used a sin to keep us in bondage in the past, he will use it again and again until we allow Christ to break those bonds by choosing to walk in the freedom He died to provide. His death and resurrection broke the bonds. Forever. It has become my choice to then walk in His freedom or under the enemy's yoke of fear.

When the trials come now, He has taught me to proceed without fear and to trust Him more each step of the way. This, my sisters, is a true miracle and act of His grace and mercy. He wants us to enjoy freedom from fear. He wants us to trust Him—no matter what. He wants us to trust that His plan is perfect and His will is irrefutably best. He wants us to obey His command to not let our hearts be troubled. We can have His peace.

I can't heal a weak limb for Sydney, but He can. I can't meet all of our financial needs or the needs of my children, but He can. I can't defeat the enemy and refute his lies in my own strength, but I can through God and His authoritative Word. I'm so glad to be on His side and covered in the shelter of His wings. I'm so glad the enemy is powerless against me if I do not let him have access to my mind. I am thrilled to know and comforted beyond measure that whatever comes to me, be it an attack from the enemy or an opportunity to learn a lesson from my own failure, it has not happened without my loving Lord's awareness and permission. How could I not trust this Jesus?

The fires will purify and refine your character. He doesn't just want to refine the gold in your life. He wants to consume your *dross*. Dross is scum on molten metal, refuse, rubbish. Do you have a little scum in your life you'd like to have removed? How about getting rid of the refuse or rubbish that's cluttering your mind, heart, and testimony? God's removal process may not always please you, but the end result will be a beautiful, refined piece of gold you can one day lay before His precious throne. He loves you this much. He longs for you to be this pure. Our God is a consuming fire. Let Him burn up your failures in the past and your fears in the present. Yield to Him when the furnace of circumstances seems too painful to withstand. You can trust Him. He has a plan, and it is perfect. Let Him consume all that He must so that you can radiate all that He is.

# Fast Food for Thought

- ☞ What do you understand about the faithfulness of God? How have you been able to live it out?

- ☞ Do you really know God's Word and can you recall it by memory if you need to do spiritual battle for yourself and others? What steps are you willing to take to learn His Word better?

🔥 How are you doing trusting God through the fire? Would you share what He has done for you?

🔥 Can you decide now that the next time the fire rages, you will be still and let the Lord fight for you, all the while trusting and praising His name?

*Dear Jesus, I am so thankful that I never have to go through any trial, test, or fire without you. Help me be fearless, and help me wait for you to deliver me with praise on my lips to the one faithful, true God who will never leave me or forsake me. You are my strength, and I am always safe because of you. Thank you for your limitless faithfulness and all of your provisions. Thank you that you always love me and always work on my behalf and that nothing can separate me from you. Thank you for your Word, which is my blueprint for life. I love you. In your name I pray, amen.*

## CHAPTER 11

# Fasting to See What Really Matters

*A*s Christians, we are not of this world. We are citizens of heaven (Phil. 3:20). Why then are we so attached to many aspects of this world? Why is it hard to keep our focus on exactly why we are here—to know God, to love Him and our neighbor, and to share Jesus with the world?

The apostle John tells us, "Do not love the world or anything in the world. If anyone loves the world, love for the Father is not in them. For everything in the world—the lust of the flesh, the lust of the eyes, and the pride of life—comes not from the Father but from the world. The world and its desires pass away, but whoever does the will of God lives forever" (1 John 2:15–17).

Fasting and prayer can help us love God and what He offers far more than any temptation the world tries to lure us toward.

# From Suzanne

*Fasting and prayer have taught me that this world is quickly passing away and all that is in it will also. People are the only things on this planet that are everlasting. Prayer gives me the opportunity to pray for the salvation of the lost. Fasting has heightened the truth that this world has nothing to offer, but in Jesus we have all that we will ever need.*

Have you ever caught yourself loving the things of the world? I have. It's hard not to. Everyday we are faced with online overload, the newest toys, the latest technology and the hottest vacation spot. Several thousand media messages can bombard us every day, if we allow it. Our desires can run the cycle of a roller coaster. Add to that busy lives, a hectic pace, and a stressed-out world, and we can be a hot mess if we don't remember what our identity is in Christ is.

Jesus told us what matters most: "You shall love the Lord your God with all your heart, and with all your soul, and with all your strength, and with all your mind; and your neighbor as yourself" (Luke 10:27 NASB). And the One we are to love most, to love fully, tells what He expects from us: "To act justly and to love mercy and to walk humbly with your God" (Mic. 6:8).

This involves such acts of mercy as feeding the hungry, giving drink to the thirsty, taking care of the stranger, clothing the naked, visiting the sick and those in prison, and taking care of orphans and widows (Matt. 25:35–40; James 1:27). And, of course, our primary purpose on this earth is to "go and make disciples of all nations, baptizing them in the name of the Father and of the Son and of the Holy Spirit" (Matt. 28:19).

What would the world look like if all Christians actually lived out these directives? I believe there would be a revival the likes of which we have never seen. These are what *really* matter in life.

My family and I cared for my mom in our home when she was passing away from cancer. The cancer part was something I never wanted to experience, but taking care of my mom was something I will never regret. She was an amazing woman, some would say quirky. At ninety years of age, she wore spandex pants and hot pink, leopard fur-trimmed leather jackets, got her nails done faithfully, and dyed her gray hair blonde. She even had her eyebrows tattooed in her late eighties. She always thought that wherever we went, men much younger than her were flirting with her. She was a hoot, and everyone loved her. The fact that God allowed us to tell her every day for about a month that we loved her as she readied to go home to Him was a gift.

Holding her hand as she entered into heaven was hard yet victorious. I miss her terribly. I also know that when God told me our family was to care for her, our act of love and obedience would be something that really mattered, especially to Him. Had I not been fine-tuned to listen to His voice through prayer and fasting, I might have considered letting hospice continue to care for her. I would have missed a great blessing and the comfort that she left this world knowing how very much she was loved by our entire family.

Does your life reflect God's priorities? Are you living out what matters most? Fast and pray about this with us. Maybe then the world will come to know Christ.

# From Wendy

*Fasting and praying have taught me the truth and attainability of Paul's words to the Corinthians: "For I determined to know nothing among you except Jesus Christ, and Him crucified" (1 Cor. 2:2 NASB).*

Jesus' story is all about the Father and the Holy Spirit. It's about the universe, life itself, humanity, the Word, the cross, our redemption, our eternity. Jesus' story, paradoxically, was never all about me, yet He did it all for me. And all for you. Because of His great and unsearchable mind and the love that flows from Him.

How do we determine that we are called to be *in* and not *of* the world, to know nothing but Christ and Him crucified? Fasting is a fine-tuner! This is what I mean. You, or someone you know, may have had opportunities to go on mission trips to foreign places of high poverty. When you spend even a few short days in an environment like this, you almost feel disgusted and overwhelmed when you come out of customs at a US airport. The sights and sounds of abundance bombard you with the things of this world and the chaos to which we have grown numb. The mission trip gave you a new perspective. God caused some scales to fall from your eyes and allowed you to see life differently.

Time and time again when our students at church come back from a mission trip, they describe this experience. Now fasting will do the same to your spirit and human eyes if you let it. Seeking God through a bit of self-denial on a consistent basis allows you to view things differently. Some of the friends that seemed so fun before suddenly lose their luster. The striving for more, for bigger and better will become less desirable when it comes to material goods. You begin to hear where God may want you to bless someone else with a meal or a financial gift, and it will become your great delight to do it and give it.

That is the amazing secret of walking with God: the fine scalpel He uses to do surgery on our hearts and minds is often painless. Some of the *circumstances* are so painful they are only survivable by His grace, that's true. But the actual cutting away of what doesn't belong and the infusing of His spirit into those places are a joy. Since the circumstances are going to come regardless, why not let them be used by God to focus your heart and mind on what truly matters to Him for your life and your legacy? You are leaving a legacy of faith or of wandering. What is your prayer for your children? For your children's children? For your extended family? For your friends and acquaintances? Be sure *you* live in a way that matches what you pray for. How you live for Christ is your legacy.

I love the world God created. I love its beauty and the fun to be found in it. It's an exciting place, and I know God wants us to enjoy it. For this reason, I have always walked a fine line between wanting to be in the world and not of it. That's why I want you to see that fasting really works, because it has helped me discern the difference in how I should live.

For example, I love beautiful handbags. I know a collection of expensive handbags is not God's will for me, nor should I spend time lusting for them. But this doesn't mean I can't think they are beautiful. It doesn't mean I must ignore their existence. I think God is calling women of our generation to be relevant, to be out-there-in-the-world Christians who are familiar with the music, the trends, the temptations our kids will face, and not be afraid of seeing the pretty shiny things in store windows. He just wants us to rise above it all. He will refine our desires and pursuits if we let Him. He has shown me through fasting how to be relevant and, at the same time, completely consumed by Him. If we isolate ourselves to the point that we are only surrounded by people who think and behave exactly as we do, then our spheres of influence will be very small and our light can grow very dim. We need to be in the world, ladies, just not of it.

The truth is, the woman with the expensive bag is just as much in need of Jesus as the orphan in the Third World country. We are all going to be called into places to bear His light. Some women can own and carry an expensive bag into a room and have doors opened to her for sharing the gospel that others would not. Likewise, someone entering a humble dwelling in an impoverished place in complete humility will have an opportunity for Christ that others will not. Let's not waste time judging who is closer to Christ. Instead, let's spend time at the feet of Jesus and learn His heart. And His heart's desire is that *all* come to know Him. Learn to let God's Spirit be your barometer, like Paul did, in guiding your mind as well as your ministry to others:

For though I am free from all men, I have made myself a slave to all, so that I may win more. To the Jews I became as a Jew, so that I might win Jews; … to those who are without law, as without law, though not being without the law of God but under the law of Christ, so that I might win those who are without law. To the weak I became weak, that I might win the weak; I have become all things to all men, so that I may by all means save some. (1 Cor. 9:19–23 NASB)

Don't be afraid of the world. But be wise as you go out into it, as Jesus told the disciples (Matt. 10:16). Let your continued building of faith and closeness to Him come through times of regular prayer and fasting from things of this world. But never forget, God so loved the world that He gave us His Son! The world is where the people are who need to hear your story. Focus on Him, because He *is* what really matters. Then get out there! Live!

# Fast Food for Thought

- In what ways do you struggle with being in the world and not of it? Will you let fasting from a worldly mentality be something you try? Will you ask Christ to give you a heart for those around you?

- How does your life show that God's priorities are yours, that what matters to Him matters to you?

- Do you want to be part of changing the world for

Christ? That takes living a life that shows Jesus to everyone you encounter. Are you doing that? If so, how? If not, will you commit to praying and fasting, asking Christ to help you be more like Him?

☙ Are you sharing Christ with those who don't know Him? Will you commit to praying and fasting for the lost?

*Dear Jesus, thank you that this world is not my home, so it has nothing for me to lay claim to, no desire for me to yearn for. Please help me keep my eyes fixed on you. Help me to be in this world and be used by you. But help me never be transformed by this world. Keep my thinking in line with yours. Please keep me from living in isolation and fear, and help me be bold to go out into the world, proclaiming who you are by the way I live my life. I know this is only possible through the power of your Spirit. In your name I pray, amen.*

# PART THREE

# Personalizing Your Plan

*Jesus answered, "It is written:*
*'Man shall not live on bread alone,*
*but on every word that comes from*
*the mouth of God.'"*

—JESUS CHRIST (MATT. 4:4)

## CHAPTER 12

# How to Be Fast Friends on a Fast-Paced Day

*W*e would be hard-pressed to say which thing was more difficult to do: going a day (or meal) without eating, or finding time in a hectic day to spend focused moments with Christ. Would you love to run away to a quiet place of retreat with your Bible and little else? Have you dreamed of this? We have.

My (Wendy's) ideal getaway would be in Ireland. Green hills rolling down to the sea and me in a thatched-roof cottage sitting by a fire with my Bible and a notebook. It would be raining, I would have a pot of tea, and sheep would be dotting the hillside.

My (Suzanne's) ideal retreat would be much different than Wendy's. I crave excitement, bright lights, sunny beaches, and tropical locales. Some of that fits with Times Square in New York City. The rest with Hawaii. If I could have Hawaiian beaches during the day and Times Square at night, I would have my perfect getaway.

Of course, we both know that ideals are idyllic, so they

rarely happen. All of us have to live in the everyday world. And in today's world, we are busier than ever with appointments, meetings, schedules, and practices. There is a different schedule for each person in the house, or if you are single, for each day of the week. What many of us would like most of all on any given day is a nap! In spite of all the busyness, we encourage you to keep a set appointment time with God daily and to make prayer and fasting a priority. If this just seems like one more impossible thing to do, take heart. We need to let you in on a great truth: *God wants to spend time with you far more than you will ever desire to spend time with Him.* He gives you the life and sustenance you need each day, and He is certainly capable of multiplying your time and energy when He knows you want to give yourself to Him. Remember, He loves you and wants to tell you things that are meant for your heart alone. Isn't that thrilling to know? The wonderful, marvelous, omnipotent God of the universe is waiting patiently and excitedly for you to make time to meet with Him today. He is available. We, on the other hand, are usually not.

Through fasting and prayer, you can focus your heart and mind on God and His precious voice through His Word and His Spirit. Fasting will help you listen more carefully to His still, small voice. Even during the hectic times. If you have an incredibly busy life, be encouraged. Many times when we have been fasting, we know He has actually spoken to us through hectic circumstances.

With this in mind, we want to share with you some creative ways to make days of fasting special times with God, even when your day seems to conspire against that. See if any of the following suggestions fit your personality or schedule better than others. You might try several or come up with something even more creative and better suited to fit your needs.

- Get up a half hour earlier on your day of fasting to be alone with God before the hectic pace of the day unfolds.

- Put on some praise music and worship God during the time you would normally spend eating breakfast.

- On the way to work, take advantage of each red light to pray for your Fast Friend's requests.

- Take a walk during lunch and praise God for His creation and the creativity in what you see. Ask Him to bless you with ways to creatively bless Him.

- Choose a memory verse for the day. Each time you feel a pang of hunger, pray first, then try to recite your memory verse. This way, you will be feeding on His Word throughout the day.

- When you feel irritated by something or some-one, ask the Lord to keep you from sinning and to refine whatever is in your personality that just got annoyed.

- If you are at home and are doing chores, pray for the people in your home who slept in the beds, wore the clothes, ate the meals, and made the messes you are now cleaning.

# From Suzanne

*Fasting and prayer have taught me that communing with God is a continual act. I can talk to God anywhere, anytime, and say anything. It is all-important for this branch to stay connected to Him, the vine.*

My life has always been busy. Today it is busier than ever. My work keeps me traveling quite often. I sometimes interview celebrities for online magazines. Nicki is getting married soon, Travis is working on his masters in theology degree, and Tyler and Alyssa gave us our first grandson. Oh, yes, and at this moment, we are still writing this book!

I have felt like a rat running on a wheel that won't stop, though I have become a happy rat. At one point I bemoaned whether or not this was normal or if I was pushing myself too hard. All of a sudden God brought to mind the verse "Do you not know that in a race all the runners run, but only one gets the prize? Run in such a way as to get the prize. Everyone who competes in the games goes into strict training. They do it to get a crown that will not last, but we do it to get a crown that will last forever" (1 Cor. 9:24). I realized God was telling me that I am running in this race until He takes me home, and He will supply all I need to finish strong—as long as I stay connected to Him. That doesn't mean I won't have vacations or other times for play and rest. But I will continue to serve God to the fullest until He is done with His earthly plan for me.

As for my fasting days, I believe I should do my best to keep those days as clear as possible, even when I have to work.

This might look like taking time with God during those minutes I would have spent eating meals and saying quick prayers throughout the day. God knows the season of the race that I am in, and He honors it. In fact, He honors any way you come to Him seeking more of Him.

## From Wendy

*Fasting and prayer have changed my life, providing me with a continual sense of God's presence and an open channel of communication with Him at all times.*

Like Suzanne, I also have a busy life. I own and run my own business, I have a phone that never stops beeping, pinging, or ringing, and I have a full family life on top of all that. Sydney is in high school and busy with voice lessons, guitar, piano, writing, and school. Robby is a sixth grader busy with Little League, school, friends, and computer games. Still, over not much time, fasting and prayer have become habits now easily adapted into my life. The same can happen for you, especially if you have a friend to share the journey with you.

I told Suzanne that without her partnership and accountability on this journey, I probably would have persisted in weekly praying and fasting for about three weeks or less. Having a sister in Christ pray for my deepest needs, fears, and failures has been one of the greatest gifts and blessings of my life. And it has been one of my greatest privileges to pray for hers.

I am excited for you to see how God can fill your fast-paced day to all fullness with more of Himself than you ever dreamed possible.

# FAST FOOD FOR THOUGHT

- ⟳ You will never have time for Jesus unless you make it a priority. He is always there for you. Will you devote time to Him daily and let Him shower His love and blessings on you?

- ⟳ Just like the little boy in the Bible who brought a few loaves of bread and fish to Jesus (John 6:9–14), God will take whatever time and sacrifice you are able to bring Him and multiply it greatly. Will you trust Him and bring Him a sacrifice of time for prayer and fasting and then see how He will bless it?

- ⟳ Consider the suggestions for fasting given to you earlier in this chapter. Take one or two and try them for a day. Ask the Lord to help make them fruitful for you.

*Dear Jesus, you have carefully ordained each one of my days. You know how full they are going to be before I even open my eyes. Please go before me and show me the moments you have for you and I to be together today. I don't want to miss a single blessing. Thank you that no matter when or where, day or night, you are always there ready to receive me. You amaze me, and I love you. In your name I pray, amen.*

## CHAPTER 13

# How to Prepare for Your Fasting Day

*W*e are both spontaneous women who like to take life as it happens. We like to be ready for fun and any opportunity at a moment's notice. However, to enter into this kind of fasting and committed prayer time, we had to have a little organization. We agreed on a few procedures to make our fasting days have some order. What we suggest below is based on what we do, but we also encourage you to seek God on how you want to partner.

Set a day to be your Fast Friend day—a day you are sure will usually work for you on a weekly basis, knowing that sometimes you may need to adjust it. Be as consistent as you can; otherwise, you will find yourself getting too free and loose with your Fast Friend day and may have trouble sticking with it. Try your best to limit activities on that day, but do what needs to be done.

Decide how you will exchange specific requests. We chose texting and email with the occasional SOS text sent if we needed to pray together by phone.

Make a list of any prayer requests that are consistent—for example, praying that your children will have wisdom, discernment, and favor from the Lord. This will be something you can pray on all fast days or that God may even bring to mind at other prayer times during the week. Remember to add praises and thanksgivings.

Be vulnerable. This is the person God has given you to bare your soul. It is always your choice on how open you want to be. At the same time, remember that we are told in Scripture to confess our sins to one another (James 5:16) and bear one another's burdens (Gal. 6:2).

Decide what you will and will not consume. For example, we usually have coffee on our fasting days. You may want to restrict yourself to water. We sometimes knew that juices or other liquids would be needed for certain days. For us, it worked to be a little flexible in this area.

Rejoice together! For as you seek God, you will find Him and your life will never be the same again. It will be far better!

Concerning what to pray for during your Fast Friend day, we would like to offer the following suggestions. Pray …

## 1. For Each Other

- For spiritual growth through fasting
- For supernatural help in fasting
- For a hunger to know God more intimately
- For a greater love for Jesus
- For an always-growing faith
- To be the wife, friend, sister, mom, and/or employee that people in your life need you to be

- For health
- Too hear God's voice
- To be aware of sin in your life
- To be protected from the evil one
- To share your faith boldly
- For wisdom, discernment, and favor
- To be a servant—to see the needs of others and meet them

## 2. For Your Families

- For specific needs for each other's husband and children
- Pray specific Scripture over your husbands and children
- For the needs of extended family members
- You may also tailor the "For Each Other" prayer section to your husband and children

## 3. For Others

- For your friends, your church, and your community
- For your country and government
- For persecuted Christians throughout the world
- For the lost and those reaching out to them
- For the church worldwide or in certain geographical areas

# OUR PRAYER FOR YOU

We may not know you personally or even know your name, but God has birthed a love in our hearts for you. We pray for you. In fact, we started praying for you as we wrote this book. We spent time together in worship and prayer, and we specifically asked God to draw you into a fast-friend relationship that would result in a more intimate and powerful life lived for Jesus Christ. We are invested in you, and we have committed to continue praying for you. Our desire is that you fall in love all over again with Jesus Christ or even for the first time. We pray that your love for Him grows in huge proportions and results in a testimony that will share the love of Christ with many others. We believe the perfect way to end this book is to pray for you now. Will you join us?

*Dear Jesus, we pray for these precious loved ones of yours who desire to know you in the most intimate way possible. We pray that you will draw them to yourself in such a way that they insatiably crave more and more of you. We pray they will find joy in such small sacrifices in fasting, and that you will multiply back to them a huge blessing of your Spirit. Let this process change and refine them as it continues to change and refine us. We pray that their homes, their friends, their workplaces, and their churches will be impacted eternally because of the transformation of their lives. We pray over them this portion of Scripture:*

For this reason we kneel before you Father, from whom every family in heaven and on earth derives its name. I pray that out of his glorious riches he may strengthen you with power through his Spirit in your inner being, so that Christ may dwell in your hearts through faith. And I pray that you, being rooted and established in love, may have power, together with all the Lord's holy people, to grasp how wide and long and high and deep is the love of Christ, and to know this love that surpasses knowledge—that you may be filled to the measure of all the fullness of God. Now to him who is able to do immeasurably more than all we ask or imagine, according to his power that is at work within us, to him be glory in the church and in Christ Jesus throughout all generations, for ever and ever! (Eph. 3:14–21)

*In your name we pray, amen.*

# Fast Friends

## 10-WEEK BOOK STUDY

# Finding Your Fast Friend

*Week 1:* Read Chapters 1–3

*For he satisfies the thirsty and fills the hungry with good things.*
(Psalm 107:9 NIV)

We love food. That's why fasting is a genuine sacrifice for us. A fun Friday night for Wendy is to sit on a comfy couch with a stack of cookbooks or Pinterest recipes to browse. Better yet with Ina Garten, aka "Barefoot Contessa," on in the background. For years Suzanne fed a family of five with a revolving door open to all of their kids' hungry friends. She became creative and innovative on her own, and can stretch a recipe for five to accommodate a housefull.

We have created a how-to section on fasting using a recipe format that does not include food. Each recipe has a few simple ingredients and easy to follow instructions. These recipes are for you to determine how to tailor your day or season of fasting. We encourage you to use them with your "Fast Friend," but can be used on your own as well.

*What you will need:*

- Time in prayer seeking the Lord on the right "Fast Friend" as your partner. Listen for His voice and when you believe He has revealed the person to you, pray for her before you approach her that God will reveal his will to her also.
- If it takes a while to find a Fast Friend, don't get discouraged. God's timing is perfect. He will connect you to the right person at the right time. Just stay in tune with God.
- Once your Fast Friend has accepted your invitation, seek God together on the basics.

*The Basics*

- Choose a day that works for both of you.
- Seek the Lord for what type of fast is best for you and your "Fast Friend."

- Share your prayer requests the day prior to fasting by phone, text, or email.

- Find a place you will use as your "prayer closet."

- Have your Bible, worship music, and a journal.

- Pray and study the Word.

- Become familiar with a concordance or a resource that lets you search your Bible to find verses that apply to each topic.

- Begin to commit the "recipe card" Scriptures to memory.

- Pray individually but also pray together as God leads.

*Ingredients for effective fasting*
*and a healthy Fast Friend relationship:*

- Commitment: Be committed to Christ and your Fast Friend. You have entered into an agreement with your Fast Friend to be there to support her with fervent prayer.

- Confidentiality: You must keep everything confidential unless one of you asks that a request be shared for prayer support from others also.

- Repentant heart: Be ready to confess any sin and receive the gift of God's forgiveness.

- Humility: Be humble before God and man.

- Worship: Worship the Lord using prayer, music, and journaling with your sacrifice.

- Gratitude: Be thankful in all things, even when you don't see the answer yet; in fact, thank God ahead of time for the answer he will provide!

- Intercessory prayer: Be an intercessor for your Fast Friend, her family, others in your lives, your church, our country, and the world.

- Faith: Ask God for great faith. Trust in Him and be confident in who your God is and what He can do.

As you do this study, make sure to answer all of the questions at the end of each chapter and discuss your thoughts. As you pray for each other's lives, families, and needs, your pantry will begin to overflow with hope, answered prayer, increased faith, and an intimate relationship with God. We believe this will bear fruit in your life and the lives of your loved ones. You will be known as the woman of faith in your family and the friend to seek for intercessory prayer. Follow this recipe for prayer and fasting. *It will bring nourishment to your soul, health to your heart, and create a hunger and thirst that can only be satisfied by more time in the presence of your Savior!*

# *Fast Friend Recipe*
## TO CONFESS SIN

*Week 2:* Read Chapter 4

*If we confess our sin, He is faithful and just to forgive our sin and cleanse us from all unrighteousness.* (1 John 1:9 NASB)

We need to reflect on and repent of sin in our lives. As high priests in Christ (1 Peter 2:5), we can also intercede for the sins of our country. The Holy Spirit will reveal areas that need confession in your life, for others and our land.

At times, we feel deeply convicted by sin. God forgives. We need to accept His forgiveness and extend forgiveness to others. To grow in our relationship with Jesus and be used by Him, we must confess, accept forgiveness, thank God for it and move forward. Scripture states Jesus' blood covers our sin and cleanses our *consciences.* Because of His sacrificial death and resurrection, we can draw near to Him (Hebrews 10:22) and have our conscience cleansed from dead works to serve the living God (Hebrews 9:14).

*Ingredients:*
- Contrite and broken spirit
- Confession of sin to God
- Desire for true repentance
- Willingness to receive God's grace and forgiveness

True repentance turns to Jesus with a sorrowful heart and desire for change. Take time this week to repent. You may also need to make amends with someone you may have wronged. This could manifest as confessing your sins to one another. Pray for humility, vulnerability, wisdom, and compassion towards each other. *The baking process is not pleasant, but the end result will be a sweet aroma to the Father and others.*

# *Fast Friend Recipe*
## FOR OBTAINING GOD'S GUIDANCE

*Week 3:* Read Chapter 5

*Make me know Your ways O Lord; teach me Your paths, Lead me in Your truth and teach me, for You are the God of my salvation; for You I wait all the day. (*Psalms 25:4–5 NASB)

We are to be students of God's Word. Second Timothy 2:15 says to work at knowing God's word of truth, handling it correctly. Revelation 22:18 shares that if anyone adds anything to God's Word, there are definite consequences. Consistent prayer, meditating on Scripture, and sharing the Word with others is our calling in life as a Christ-follower. Make it a habit to seek God for all decisions in life, big and small. He is the one who ultimately chooses our path, for "the mind of man plans his way, but the Lord directs his steps" Proverbs 16:9 (NIV).

*Ingredients:*
- A regular time to study God's Word daily
- A heart of obedience
- Prayer for wisdom and discernment
- Desire to please God by following His instructions

Those who love God naturally want to follow His directives. Confusion is not from the Lord; it is from the enemy. Pray to clearly discern the voice of your Savior. God will always lead you if you ask Him. Seek Him, find Him, obey Him, know His Word so you can truthfully share it with others, and live abundantly, believing that He is giving you the wisdom His Word promises in James 1:5. *Pare away your plan and follow God's guidance.*

# *Fast Friend Recipe*
## FOR WORSHIP

*Week 4:* Read Chapter 6

*Bless the Lord, O my soul; and all that is within me, bless His holy name. Bless the Lord, O my soul, and forget none of His benefits.* (Psalm 103:1, 2 NASB)

Sometimes there is nothing sweeter than to praising God for who He is and what He has done. When days are hectic, we rarely forget to make our requests made known to God. Intentionally taking time to praise, thank, and worship Him is a refreshing change of pace for many of us and our prayer lives. If this is a new experience for you, try opening to Psalms and begin to declare out loud the praises sung by His peoples for thousands of years. You will soon discover the Holy Spirit leading you in worship of your own.

*Ingredients:*
- Bible and a quiet space
- Journal to record favorite verses/praises
- Worship music
- A choice to put aside all worries and distractions

His praises will free your heart and mind from burdens of fear and despair. It blesses God to hear our praises. Start every day of fasting with praise and worship to the King. Let hunger pangs remind you to "forget none of His benefits." Praise His holiness, righteousness, salvation, love, and continue with a list of your own. *Let His attributes take root in your life, producing a fruit-of-the-Spirit ambrosia so amazing, your friends will be begging for the recipe.*

# *Fast Friend Recipe*
## FOR YOUR HUSBAND AND MARRIAGE

*Week 5:* Read Chapter 7

*However, each one of you also must love his wife as he loves himself, and the wife must respect her husband.* (Ephesians 5:33 NIV)

In marriage, two become one flesh. Treat each other well as the number one person in your lives. Pray daily for your husband and marriage. Ask him what he needs prayer for and tell him your requests. Pray together if possible. If your spouse is not a believer, pray all the more that God opens his eyes to the truth. *Always* respect your husband. Never fight or put each other down to or in front of others. Respect goes both ways and showing it to one another results in love and a successful union.

*Ingredients:*

- Keep Jesus as your first love
- Desire to honor the name of Christ by working towards a godly marriage
- Love your spouse by praying for him, serving him, honoring him, respecting him, and being his #1 fan
- Minister to your spouse as your husband and brother in Christ

If you are not married yet, pray and wait in faith, trusting God with your future. If your husband has been unfaithful or personally harmed you, seek counsel. God hates adultery and abuse and wants you to get the help you need.

Marriage is an example of Christ and His church. Your wedding day vow was before the Lord: protect it and work at it with every ounce of strength you have. *Garnish every act with love.*

# Fast Friend Recipe
## FOR THE LIVES OF YOUR CHILDREN

*Week 6:* Read Chapter 8

*These words, which I am commanding you today, shall be on your heart. You shall teach them diligently to your sons and shall talk of them when you sit in your house and when you walk by the way and when you lie down and when you rise up. (Deuteronomy 6:6–7)*

Whatever you want your children to be, *be that*! Live your testimony in Christ before them. Your greatest goal for them is salvation in Jesus Christ. Proverbs 22:6 promises that if you teach them the ways of the Lord, even if they stray, they will return. We see Timothy's mother's faithfulness in 2 Timothy 3:15, how from infancy she taught him the holy Scriptures to make him wise to lead him to salvation in Christ Jesus.

*Ingredients:*

- Pray Scripture over your children
- Pray for godly qualities, wisdom, discernment, and that their heart will be completely His
- Find teachable moments in daily occurrences
- Love them, discipline them, forgive them, and show them the mercy God shows you

Seek God on decisions that need to be made on behalf of your child. Do not rush to solve a situation without petitioning the Holy Spirit. God has entrusted this child to you and will hold you accountable. It is a precious, incredible privilege to mold a child and a tremendous responsibility before God. *Add sugar in the form of kisses, hugs, and encouragement!*

# *Fast Friend Recipe*
## TO BREAK BONDAGE

*Week 7:* Read Chapter 9

*The weapons we fight with are not the weapons of the world.*
*On the contrary, they have divine power to demolish strongholds.*
(2 Corinthians 10:4 NIV)

God wills us to experience freedom from sin. In Isaiah, God doesn't say He desires *some* bands to be broken, but to break *every yoke*. Grasp the power of this and believe that the effective prayers of the righteous accomplish much (James 5:16). Experience victory in your lives and in the lives of your loved ones by praying in faith the name and blood of Christ to destroy strongholds. In Hebrews 12:4, we are reminded we have not yet resisted to the point of shedding blood in our striving against sin. To break the power of addictions or habitual sins will require absolute repentance on our part including a commitment to change. God's resurrection power is available to us through the power of His Spirit, to make us more than conquerors in Christ!

*Ingredients:*

- Thoughts consciously taken captive to Christ
- Desire to die to old self and put on the new
- Intentional practice of new habits
- Intercessory prayer

Jesus paid for our freedom through His blood. This sacrifice on His part should stir in us a desire to live as the redeemed children we are. Pray fervently for this freedom for yourself and for those you love! *Sift away defeat and let the power of Christ rise in you!*

# Fast Friend Recipe
## TO STRENGTHEN YOUR FAITH

*Week 8:* Read Chapter 10

*Stand firm in your faith or you will not stand at all.*
(Isaiah 7:9b NIV)

Jesus promised us that in this life we would have struggles, but not to dismay because He has overcome and we will also by the blood of the Lamb! Hebrews 11:6 says that without faith it is impossible to please God, and James 1:6–7 advises us to believe and not doubt, for if we doubt we will not receive anything from the Lord. Consider how powerfully, faithfully, and miraculously *able* our God is and stake your life on it. When the arrows of our enemy are launched, take courage from James 4:7, which promises if we resist the devil he *will* flee from us.

*Ingredients:*
- Faith of a mustard seed
- Belief in who God is, what he can do, speaking life into your situation
- Gratitude in advance for his deliverance
- Persistent prayer

Take your negative thoughts captive by countering them with truth from God's Word. Pray with power through Christ to break down any strongholds or lies and *refuse* to let them take root in your life. Romans 5:3–4 will assure you the good that tribulation, perseverance, and proven character bring. God is in control. For He has a perfect plan which includes hope and a future (Jeremiah 29:11) and all things working together for good to those who know him and love him (Romans 8:28). *Combine all of these ingredients for victory in Christ.*

# Fast Friend Recipe
## TO SEE WHAT REALLY MATTERS IN LIFE

*Week 9:* Read Chapter 11

*But seek first His kingdom and His righteousness; and all these things shall be added unto you. (*Matthew 6:33 NASB)

As women, beginning with the end in mind is an area where we excel. We are often big-picture thinkers with the ability to execute a plan. We can use this to vision-cast a Christ-centered life for those around us. We have more eyes on us than we realize, watching our choices, priorities, and responses. What a responsibility to show others we live seeking His kingdom first, and trusting Him for the "all these things." Take frequent inventories on fasting days. Ask the Spirit to reveal areas you are realigning your thinking with the world and not the Word.

*Ingredients:*

- A trusting heart. *He will meet all your needs according to His riches in glory.*
- A willing mind. *Ask for His eyes to see issues and options before you.*
- An obedient disposition. *What He tells you to abandon, abandon!*
- An observable joy. *Peace should rule and result from your obedience.*

Your home will be transformed. You will live out a life that shows His power and glory. If you struggle with a particular need or lure, there is no better source for wisdom than His Word. Search Scripture like you are mining for great treasure, because you are! *Let Jesus become your Bread of Life, served with an unending supply of Living Water.*

# Fast Friend Recipe
## TO RUN THE RACE AND FINISH STRONG

*Week 10:* Read Chapters 12 and 13

*And let us not be weary in well doing: for in due season we shall reap, if we faint not.* (Galatians 6:9 KJV)

Isn't it comforting to know we serve a God whose mercies are new every morning? A God who recognizes when we are exhausted, despairing, stumbling on a wrong path, or just trying to find our way in a desert? We can approach the throne of grace of the God of all creation, and call Him *Abba*! We do not serve a God who is tapping His foot in impatience, arms crossed, giving us a look of disapproval if we fail. We serve a God who loves us beyond measure and who sings over us. When you have pressed on, as you have through these weeks of prayer and fasting, we know you have experienced many victories and a few failures. We did and still do! To do well and continue on without growing faint, we have a few tips.

*Ingredients:*

- A heaping portion of grace for yourself and others
- A steady infilling of Scripture for encouragement and guidance
- Frequent pinches of laughter and fun with your Fast Friend
- The power of His Spirit for energy and stamina

With the right combination of these ingredients, you will be able to push past any plateaus or stumbles you may experience. *This recipe feeds two with plenty of strength and joy for the journey!*

# Concluding Your Book Study

*And they overcame him (Satan) because of the blood of the Lamb and because of the word of their testimony, and they did not love their life even when faced with death.* (Revelation 12:11 NASB)

By this point, we hope you have been forever changed by this season of fasting and prayer. We want you to know that we have been praying for you. If this book is in your hands, we have asked the Lord to take you into a love relationship and spiritual life with Him that is beyond your wildest dreams. We won't be surprised if this "*season*" actually turns into a lifestyle for you as it has for us.

At times in our lives, between our day jobs, families, friends, our church and ministry activities, and the various and sundry other things that engulf our time, we can get weary. We can easily feel that way about the race we are running. God gently reminds us that the race doesn't end as long as we are on this earth.

The Great Commission, to which God has called all believers, is a lifetime assignment. Just because we are busy, we don't stop living a full life of surrender to Christ nor take a vacation from sharing the gospel. Coming to terms with the fact that this "race" will continue until God welcomes us home can give us a new, energized perspective. If Christ has called us to this, He will give us the strength to complete it. Matthew 25:21 talks about a master commending his good and faithful servant for a job well done. Doesn't your heart yearn to hear that from your Lord?

We encourage you, as we do ourselves, to ask Jesus to help you run like you have never run before. Run with a renewed vision, passion, hunger for Him and His Word, boldness to share the truth of the gospel, and complete, unequivocal dedication.

If you get tired, rest in your Lord and let Him fill you up. If you feel weak, remember that is when He is strong. And on those days when you are pondering the truth that this world is not your home and that you will stand before the Lord one day, think about finishing the race with excellence. One day, you *will* cross the finish line and run into the arms of your Savior. Run...because on that day, there is nothing more you will want to hear than Him proclaim, "Well done, good and faithful servant." *Amen!*

# About the Authors

*Suzanne Niles* is the public relations and media representative for The Salvation Army Vision Network. Suzanne has worked in different facets of the entertainment business for several decades, including acting, producing, and arranging promotions through all types of media outlets. She has a passion for Jesus, networking and connecting people to the proper cause. Suzanne makes her home in Spokane, Washington.

*Wendy Simpson Little* is the owner and broker of a small real estate company in Central California. In her previous careers, she has been a stay at home mom, and taught seventh grade English and high school French. She has a passion for her friends and family, fun and life! She hopes to encourage other women in faith, prayer, and a love for God and his Word. Wendy makes her home in Visalia, California.